JOSSEY-BASS TEACHER

Jossey-Bass Teacher provides educators with practical knowledge and tools to create a positive and lifelong impact on student learning. We offer classroom-tested and research-based teaching resources for a variety of grade levels and subject areas. Whether you are an aspiring, new, or veteran teacher, we want to help you make every teaching day your best.

From ready-to-use classroom activities to the latest teaching framework, our value-packed books provide insightful, practical, and comprehensive materials on the topics that matter most to K–12 teachers. We hope to become your trusted source for the best ideas from the most experienced and respected experts in the field.

For more information about our resources, authors, and events please visit us at: www.josseybasseducation.com.

You may also find us on Facebook, Twitter, and Pinterest.

 Jossey-Bass K-12 Education

 jbeducation

Pinterest jbeducation

The Literacy Cookbook

The Literacy Cookbook

A PRACTICAL GUIDE TO EFFECTIVE
READING, WRITING, SPEAKING,
AND LISTENING INSTRUCTION

Sarah Tantillo

With illustrations by
Sandy Gingras

JOSSEY-BASS
A Wiley Imprint
www.josseybass.com

Cover design: Jeff Puda
Cover images © Getty

Published by Jossey-Bass
A Wiley Imprint
One Montgomery Street, Suite 1200, San Francisco, CA 94104-4594—www.josseybass.com

Jossey-Bass books and products are available through most bookstores. To contact Jossey-Bass directly call our Customer Care Department within the U.S. at 800-956-7739, outside the U.S. at 317-572-3986, or fax 317-572-4002.

Wiley publishes in a variety of print and electronic formats and by print-on-demand. Some material included with standard print versions of this book may not be included in e-books or in print-on-demand. If this book refers to media such as a CD or DVD that is not included in the version you purchased, you may download this material at **http://booksupport.wiley.com**. For more information about Wiley products, visit **www.wiley.com**.

Library of Congress Cataloging-in-Publication Data
Tantillo, Sarah, 1965–
   A practical guide to effective reading, writing, speaking, and listening instruction / Sarah Tantillo; with illustrations by Sandy Gingras.
      p. cm.
   Includes bibliographical references and index.
   ISBN 978-1-118-28816-0 (pbk.)
   ISBN 978-1-118-33376-1 (ebk.)
   ISBN 978-1-118-33153-8 (ebk.)
   ISBN 978-1-118-33489-8 (ebk.)
   1. Reading. I. Title.
   LB1050.T33 2012
   418′.4—dc23
                          2012030716

504/ 3821   0½3

Printed in the United States of America
FIRST EDITION

PB Printing   10 9 8 7 6 5 4 3 2 1

ABOUT THE AUTHOR

Sarah Tantillo consults with schools (especially urban schools) seeking to improve student achievement. She taught high school English and humanities in both suburban and urban New Jersey public schools for fourteen years, including seven years at the high-performing North Star Academy Charter School of Newark, New Jersey, where she chaired the Humanities Department and her students achieved a 100 percent passing rate on the High School Proficiency Assessment (HSPA) for Language Arts and Literacy. In addition to teaching, she also founded the New Jersey Charter School Resource Center and the New Jersey Charter Public Schools Association. She led the Resource Center from 1996 to 1999 and the Association from 1999 to 2003. Since 2007, she has coached K–12 schools on literacy instruction, curriculum development, data-driven instruction, school culture-building, and strategic planning. In 2009, she launched The Literacy Cookbook Website (http://www.literacycookbook.com) to provide teachers and school leaders with practical resources and strategies for literacy instruction. That Website formed the basis for this book. In her free time, she writes a blog called Only Good Books (http://onlygoodbooks.wordpress.com). Tantillo earned her B.A. from Princeton University, her M.Ed. from Harvard University, an M.A. from Johns Hopkins University, and her Ed.D. from Rutgers University.

ACKNOWLEDGMENTS

This book represents a culmination of several decades of fortunate educational experiences combined with a lifelong obsession with what it takes to read and write well. Since the day I entered first grade, when my teacher, Mrs. Scholl, told us that her father named her Jewel because she was so precious, "and that is how I think of all of you, as my little Jewels," so many teachers have blessed me with their expertise, enthusiasm, and love. Whether I was their student or colleague, they made deeper impressions than they probably realized, and I hope they see that now. I am also grateful to the thousands of students I have been lucky enough to work with and learn from. So many people have informed my thinking that I cannot name them all. Please picture me bowing here with gratitude.

I also recognize that I would be nowhere without the support of my family and friends, whose wit and wisdom buoyed me through this process. Again, while the list of those who deserve thanks is impossibly long, a few simply must be named. At many pivotal moments, Norman Atkins has invited me to dive into meaningful, instructive work (at North Star, TeacherU, and Relay), and I am thankful that he referred me to the wonderful folks at Jossey-Bass, especially Kate Gagnon, Tracy Gallagher, Robin Lloyd, and Sarah Miller, who have made this experience remarkably pleasant. And I am in awe of Jeff Puda for designing such a beautiful cover.

For many years, Sandy Gingras has been the proverbial stalwart ally, and I am thrilled to include her humorous illustrations in this book. PS: Sandy has written and illustrated more than twenty books, and her work can be found at the How to Live Website (http://www.how-to-live.com). Three other friends provided invaluable feedback as I was drafting this manuscript—Steve Chiger, Rahshene Davis, and Katy Wischow—and I am grateful for their insights.

Last but definitely not least, I want my parents to know how much I appreciate their continuous encouragement, generosity, and support. They made countless sacrifices so that I could get a good education. I hope it was worth it.

PART TWO Entrées

PREFACE

Like any other avid reader, I used to think I knew a lot about reading. But most of those times I was wrong. I did well in high school and went to Princeton and thought I knew how to read: wrong. Graduated with a degree in comparative literature and was sure I knew what good readers do: again, wrong. Sure, I knew how to analyze poems, stories, novels, and plays. If pressed, I could translate Baudelaire. But on the day I started teaching high school English, I realized it didn't matter. After all of that schooling, I didn't know what to do with students who struggled to read.

Like many high school teachers, I'd expected students to know how to read by the time they reached me. Wasn't that the rule? Since I'd always loved reading, I had no idea what their problems were, much less how to solve them. Entering the classroom in 1987 through the Alternate Route, I had *no* training in how to teach reading and very little in how to teach writing.

As a result, when my students were confused, I was equally baffled. But I was determined to figure out how to help them.

So I did what I usually do to solve problems: I *read* about them and tried to apply what I was learning. Over time—far too long for some students, who suffered through numerous experiments with remarkable patience—I learned enough about reading and writing to be dangerous. My students passed state tests and went on to college. Based on those results, I felt like I had some useful ideas to share. So, after teaching high school for fourteen years, I left the classroom to become a literacy consultant.

That's when I began to grasp how little I truly knew.

My first clients were inner-city elementary and middle school teachers who wanted to put their students on a trajectory to college. They trusted me, since my students (from Newark, New Jersey) had all gone to college. But unlike me, they didn't expect their students to be fully formed adult readers or eloquent writers. They needed strategies. From me.

In a semipanic, I bought stacks of books, and they rescued me. They're cited throughout this book, and most are also listed in the Recommended Reading chapter. Working with teachers in dozens of schools, I tested and retested every approach I could find or create. Learning how to teach reading—comprehension, that is (I still know less than I would like to about phonics and decoding)—led me to develop ideas about What I Wish I'd Known. I created a Website called The Literacy Cookbook and began to write this book, thinking to myself, *If only I could go back and show my struggling first-year-teacher self how to teach students how to read and write more effectively.*

Alas, I cannot go back in time. But I am pleased to offer this book and the additional materials on my Website (http://www.literacycookbook.com) to you, in the hope that you might succeed with students where many, many times I failed. With nothing but the deepest humility, I submit these ideas to you and hope they help.

The Literacy Cookbook

Introduction

One day while talking with an English teacher at a low-performing high school, I asked him what his biggest challenges were. He replied that the students' writing skills were "horrible" and added, "They don't read."

I asked him, "How much of your time is spent teaching them reading skills or strategies?"

He admitted, "Not much," and said that he didn't know what to do because "they aren't motivated." Then he asked me for help.

Grateful for his invitation and having observed how tall his students were, I began with a basketball analogy: If you took a boy who'd never played basketball in his life—never played pickup, never had it in gym class—and threw him into the middle of a game, how would he feel? If he couldn't even do a layup, how "motivated" would he be? The same is true for reading. Sure, after you're born, you're supposed to be read to, but many children are not. And then when you start school, you're supposed to be taught how to read—but still some children are not. And then year after year, you struggle because no one is teaching you how to read—how to really dig into a book, how to fall in love with words—and then you get to high school and they expect you to be good at reading. And you're not. You're frustrated and your teachers are disappointed. And they aren't sure how to help you.

This scenario, sadly, is far too common, both for students and for teachers.

As one of my friends who is an English teacher recently remarked, English teachers have it hard. "The curriculum is like a big tent," he said. "There's so much in there: reading, writing, grammar, vocabulary, novels, plays, poetry . . . It's hard to decide what to do and where to spend your time. Even if they hand you a curriculum, you're not sure how to prioritize everything."

As confusing as it is for English teachers, literacy instruction is even more perplexing for teachers of other subjects. How are they supposed to teach reading and writing on top of World War II and photosynthesis? What are they supposed to do with students who don't like to read? How can they help their students comprehend the material? How can they help them write more clearly?

The purpose of this book is to provide *all* teachers (not just English teachers) with a coherent set of principles to inform their decision making around literacy instruction, including dozens of practical tools and directions—recipes, if you will—for how to teach reading, writing, speaking, and listening. The materials in this book (and on the accompanying Website) are aligned with the English Language Arts Common Core Standards and will definitely put your students on the path to college. (PS: For more information on the Common Core State Standards, see http://www.corestandards.org. Also, check out the TLC "Standards" page for the K–12 ELA Common Core Standards Tracking Sheet, which lists each grade's standards in a separate spreadsheet. A snippet of this document, which is particularly handy when writing or evaluating curriculum, appears in the Appendix of this book.)

HOW TO USE THIS BOOK

The book is divided into BASIC INGREDIENTS, ENTRÉES, and DESSERTS. Every so often you will also find a Doggie Bag of questions to take away and reflect on. These questions will help you review the material and ensure that you're on track to apply what you've learned. *Hint:* You might want to preview these questions before you read each section, as they can also provide a useful guide to key points.

Where should you start? Although you can certainly dive in anywhere, it will make the most sense if you read through the BASIC INGREDIENTS first. The ENTRÉES then show compelling ways to combine the BASIC INGREDIENTS, and they offer detailed guidance on how to help students succeed at fundamental tasks such as persuasive writing, research papers, and test preparation. The DESSERTS section includes, naturally, a scrumptious recommended reading list and the Appendix, where you'll find a handful of extra-sweet resources.

The book begins with COMPREHENSION, explaining the comprehension process, the importance of background knowledge, and the four key critical reading skills. Note that COMPREHENSION is not just about reading comprehension;

it's about comprehension in general. The "text" could be a written passage or a painting, a song, a funny smell, or even the defense on a basketball court. The comprehension process underlies everything that we do. How well we comprehend affects how much we learn in every subject.

The next basic ingredient, READING, describes what good reading entails, discusses the importance of nonfiction, identifies characteristics of different types of readers, addresses the values of independent and guided reading, and explains how to teach students to read strategically. This chapter includes an array of before-, during-, and after-reading strategies; advice on how to use textbooks more effectively; and some tips about reading workshop.

WRITING explores why we write and how to teach students how to write, period. This chapter also identifies what students struggle with the most when they write and provides solutions to these problems. It also offers an overview of writing workshop and explains how to use mentor texts and rubrics, how to teach grammar, and how to spend less time grading papers.

SPEAKING AND LISTENING explains why oral fluency matters so much and reveals how you can train students to listen and speak more effectively. It deals with logistical challenges that teachers face during class discussions and describes how to run Socratic Seminars that will have students begging for more. Also included are descriptions of two Book Talk Projects that are guaranteed to keep audiences awake and engaged.

The ENTRÉES illustrate how to teach students to write persuasively in a way that is also tasty. These chapters also show how to connect reading, writing, and test preparation and how to write your own critical reading questions. If you don't know what DBQs are, you will probably be excited to learn that you can use the DBQ (Document-Based Question) approach no matter what subject you teach. In these chapters, you will also find a Research Paper Guide, a Literary Response Paper Writing Guide, and suggestions for how to use novels in history, social studies, and science.

In short, there is something here for everyone. In fact, there is more available than what is physically here! Throughout the book, you will find references (and if you're using an e-reader, hyperlinks) to numerous additional documents available on The Literacy Cookbook Website, http://www.literacycookbook.com. The directions that follow explain how to gain access to those materials.

HOW TO USE THE LITERACY COOKBOOK WEBSITE

The Literacy Cookbook (TLC) Website offers hundreds and hundreds of documents that you can download instantly (http://www.literacycookbook.com). Plus, they are in Word format, so you can modify them easily.

This book comes with a one-time free thirty-day trial subscription and 50 percent off annual membership for those who would like to extend their access. New materials are added to the Website frequently!

To begin your one-time free trial membership, go to the TLC "Join or Renew" page: http://www.literacycookbook.com/register.php.

Then sign up (it takes less than a minute!) and enter the following code: TLCFREE.

You will receive immediate e-mail confirmation with your user name and password, which will then give you unlimited access to all of the files mentioned throughout this book, plus many more in The Download Zone. If you're reading this book with an e-reader and you're logged into the Website, simply click on the hyperlinks to instantly access any files you desire.

At the end of your free trial, you will be prompted to extend your subscription to a full year at half price. Simply click on the prompting link and sign up. You can pay by credit card in less than a minute. *Note:* If you need to pay via purchase order or check, you'll see directions on how to do that, too.

So, let's get started.

Basic Ingredients

If you read normal (food-based) cookbooks, you've probably noticed how much emphasis the authors place on using high-quality ingredients. One recommendation you see all the time is, "Always cook with wine you would be willing to drink." Although this may say something about chefs' drinking habits, the point is well taken: what you put into a meal will determine what you get out of it. The same is true for classroom instruction.

Throughout much of my teaching career, while I had a clear sense of how important it was to cook with good wine, I knew relatively little about the comprehension process or how to teach the skills involved in reading, writing, speaking, and listening. I muddled through and learned more as I went, but in retrospect I am sure I missed many opportunities to deliver lessons that were as delicious or effective as they could have been.

Some people think that excellent teachers are simply born that way. I believe they're wrong. While some individuals might possess wonderful instincts or charisma, every great teacher I've met has demonstrated a firm grasp of the content and skills that students need in order to succeed, and as my dad would say, these things are "fact-sensitive." In other words, you can learn them. You can master them. You can become great, too. The BASIC INGREDIENTS chapters will help you with that.

Comprehension

WHAT IS COMPREHENSION, AND WHY IS IT IMPORTANT?

In *When Kids Can't Read: What Teachers Can Do*, Kylene Beers calls comprehension "both a product and a process,"[1] which makes it a little tricky. You go through the process and arrive at a destination or create something. The possibilities for getting stuck or creating something imperfect are endless. But if we know how the process works, we can avoid obstacles (or overcome them), end up somewhere rewarding, and create something powerful.

Reading, writing, and oral fluency are the purest and most common expressions of comprehension. When students read, write, or speak, they are demonstrating how much they comprehend. Comprehension and literacy are thus inextricably intertwined. This explains why the Achievement Gap is, in fact, a *literacy* gap. Students who struggle to comprehend also struggle to perform in every academic area: they fail to absorb information, fail to solve problems, and fail to express ideas effectively. So here's the bottom line: no matter what grade or subject you teach, you need to understand the comprehension process and you need to teach literacy.

MY THEORY OF COMPREHENSION

I know I'm not the first person to theorize about reading comprehension. Plenty of people have written on this topic. Nevertheless, I feel compelled to share my own theory. I think of it as "Climbing the Comprehension Process Stairs."

Let me explain this more fully. And please note: this is a theory of comprehension *in general*, not just reading comprehension. It applies to listening, seeing, smelling, touching—everything you do in order to try to understand. So, you encounter a "text," and *that "text" could be a picture, a song, a sign, a book, or even the defense on a basketball court*.

As you approach the "text," the first thing you do—a thing you will repeatedly do—is access your prior knowledge or skills that relate to this "text." As illustrated in the Comprehension Process Stairs, your prior knowledge and skills might include previous experiences, the context, texts previously read

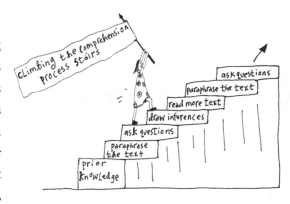

or academic content knowledge, and knowledge of conventions such as genre, grammar, and syntax. You use your prior knowledge and skills first to orient yourself to the "text," then in your initial attempt to "paraphrase" it. *In other words, you begin to use what you know to put the "text" into your own words.*

If the text involves words, you will need to unpack the vocabulary, unpack the grammar and syntax, and draw inferences from idioms. (More on paraphrasing in a moment.)

• If the "text" is a basketball game and you're a point guard dribbling up-court, you would use your prior knowledge of defenses (countless hours of practice) to observe how the defense is setting up and think, "Oh, they're playing man-to-man."

• If you're reading a story and it says, "The man fell down," you would use your prior knowledge of vocabulary to paraphrase that to "He collapsed." PS: Some people think paraphrasing means "simplifying." I prefer to think of it as "putting it in your own words, using the strongest vocabulary possible."

Once you've paraphrased this bit of "text," you immediately ask questions about it. These questions are also based on your prior knowledge and skills. Some people do this so quickly that they don't even notice they've done it. By contrast, many students don't do it very well, if at all. Why? If you lack prior knowledge and skills relating to the "text," you don't know what to ask. Also, if you struggle to paraphrase the text (if it's figuratively or literally Greek to you), it will be difficult to generate questions other than "What does *that* mean?" Even if you are able to paraphrase the text, if you don't have frequent practice in explaining things logically, you might not think of the most logical questions to ask. When people wring their hands about how "kids can't think critically," *part of the problem is that students lack background knowledge and part is that they lack experience in questioning and explaining.*

• In the case of our point guard, the most logical question would be, "Which offensive play should I call?"

• In the case of the Falling Man, you would wonder, "Why did he collapse?"

The next step—again, often done at lightning speed—is to use your prior knowledge and skills in an attempt to answer the question. If you've seen a text like this before or are highly familiar with the situation or content, the answer might be limited or obvious. Or it might require some reasoning as you sort through what you know. *The result of this thinking (also called "extended reasoning") is an inference.*

• The point guard might think, "Well, we only have three different offensive plays to use against a man-to-man defense, and the first one didn't work, so let me call our second play and see if we score."

• In wondering why the Falling Man collapsed, I would quickly recall my various experiences with falling: on basketball courts (of course), doing aikido (a martial art I tried for a few months in which the sensei told me I was "good at falling"—no doubt from basketball), falling down a flight of stairs, seeing a man have a seizure at a football game, and tripping over my sister's roller skates in our bedroom. After I generated these memories, I would reason that the "text" didn't say anything about the guy tripping over anything, and I know that healthy people don't usually fall down for no reason, so I would draw the conclusion that "he must have been sick."

The inference that we draw takes the form of an explanation, and it becomes an assumption that we hold onto—that is, part of our "prior" knowledge—until it is challenged by new information. PS: In the next section, we'll look at how inferences and explanations are two sides of the same coin.

- In the game, if the play worked, we'd use it again. If it didn't, we'd try something else the next time down the court.

- If the sentence after "The man fell down" said, "He should have bought those sneakers with the Velcro straps," you would correct your assumption. But if you don't know what *Velcro* is, you might not. Students who encounter unfamiliar vocabulary and lack word-attack skills or root knowledge tend to skip over what they don't understand. So they would continue to believe that the Falling Man was sick. Incidentally, *this problem—walking around with faulty assumptions—infects students in every subject*. In math, if you're firmly convinced that 5 times 5 is 20, even if you are able to read a word problem and set up the correct formula involving 5 times 5, you will still arrive at the wrong solution. This is why it's so important to teach *accurate* content. As Doug Lemov urges in *Teach Like a Champion*, we must be vigilant when conducting class discussions: "Right is Right. Set and defend a high standard of correctness in your classroom."[2] If we allow students to walk away with incorrect assumptions, we are setting them up for failure.

With each new bit of "text," we go through the process over and over: access prior knowledge and skills, paraphrase using this knowledge, question using this knowledge, and draw inferences.

For any given "text," all of our inferences add up to a main idea, which should be expressed as a complete sentence. In nonfiction, the main idea is an *argument* (such as, "Smoking is horrible for your health"). In fiction or narratives, the main idea is a theme or message (such as, "Some people will do crazy things for love."). One reason why so many students struggle with main idea is that they have missed inferences along the way. So their overall comprehension of the text is like a jigsaw puzzle with so many missing pieces that they can't see the Big Picture.

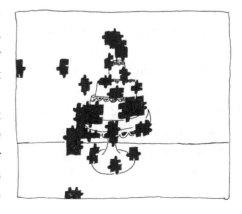

A quick note about "theme": Some people use the terms *theme* and *topic* interchangeably, and students become confused. One way to remember the difference is that topics are often single words or phrases, while themes are expressed as complete sentences. "Love" is a topic. "Love conquers all" is a theme. It's actually easier to write about a theme because you can answer the questions How? and Why? and write something compelling. Topic-oriented writing generates as much excitement as a grocery list.

For more information on theme-based writing, check out Chapter Nine, on Teaching with Novels, which includes a section on Novels in English Language Arts: Literary Response Paper Writing Guide.

WHY BACKGROUND KNOWLEDGE IS *SO* IMPORTANT

If you think about my theory of comprehension, it explains why we hear different things every time we listen to a song; why we are able to pay more attention to the use of language in, say, F. Scott Fitzgerald's *The Great Gatsby*,[3] the second or third (or fifteenth) time we read it; and why Kelly Gallagher (the author of *Deeper Reading*) and his daughters see and understand different things while watching the same baseball game.[4] The more we know about the "text," the more deeply we are able to "read" it. We bring our different experiences, skills, and knowledge to the "text" and see it through our unique lenses; we react to it in different ways. In short, our experiences shape our expectations and our actions. We look for different things and ask different questions based on what we know, so we do different things with the "text." For example, whenever I play basketball with guys, I know they'll try frantically to block my first shot, so I always fake first. But you don't need to have years of experience. If you open *Me Talk Pretty One Day* by David Sedaris[5] and the first essay makes you laugh out loud, you'll expect the rest of the essays to do the same.

Looking at it from another angle, this theory of comprehension also explains why five-year-olds can't read Russian novels. One day when I was in sixth grade, combing through my father's library, I found his copy of Dostoyevsky's *The Idiot*.[6] When I opened the book, I chuckled. As a young child, I'd circled all of the words I knew on the first few pages: mostly the words *the* and *and*. At age twelve, I tried again to read those pages and decided the book still looked too complicated. A few years later, studying it in college, I loved it. What happened?

Lacking prior knowledge (in this case, about vocabulary in general and Russian surnames in particular), children struggle to paraphrase the text. Most of their questions about *The Idiot* would be along the lines of "What does this mean? What does that mean?" and they would draw no conclusions. Having accumulated no inferences or insights, they would fail to arrive at any main idea. In short, they would have no idea what the text meant. Out of frustration, feeling stupid, they would give up.

Unfortunately, this same problem befalls many middle and high school students. It begins when they are very young. As Betty Hart and Todd R. Risley discovered, some children—from an early age—are exposed to *many* words, while others are exposed to *few*.[7] In a study of forty-two families from three different socioeconomic categories (professional, working class, and welfare), they observed and tape-recorded family interactions for an hour a month for thirty months. They found that children from the wealthiest families heard over 1,500 more words each hour, on average, than children from the poorest families (2,153 versus 616). Over a four-year period, this amounts to an estimated thirty-two-million-word gap.[8]

They also found that children mirrored their parents' vocabulary resources, use of language, and interaction styles. In fact, about nine out of every ten words in each child's vocabulary consisted of words also recorded in their parents' vocabularies.[9]

Vocabulary knowledge is clearly a key component of the background knowledge that enables comprehension. In order to paraphrase text, we must recognize words and decipher unfamiliar vocabulary. Few would dispute the correlation between vocabulary and comprehension. Indeed, Walker, Greenwood, Hart, and Carta's follow-up to Hart and Risley's study[10] of twenty-nine of the original forty-two children found that children's rate of vocabulary growth and vocabulary use at age three was strongly associated with their grade 3 standardized test scores in receptive vocabulary, listening, speaking, semantics, syntax, and reading comprehension. In short, those with a smaller vocabulary at *age* three were still struggling with reading five years later, in *grade* 3.

The problem is not merely a word gap. It's also an *explanation* gap.

Exposure to fewer words means that one hears fewer examples of complex thinking: fewer sentences, fewer questions, and fewer explanations of ideas or arguments. Hart and Risley noted that a family's language style affected the amount of language spoken because "explaining alternatives takes many more words than straightforward directives." They found that parents who explained more also asked more questions and encouraged their children to ask more questions that the parents then had to answer.[11]

In other words, children exposed to more words are also exposed to more examples of *logical thinking*. The reverse is also true. Children who communicate with others who speak less have fewer opportunities to (1) build fluency, (2) express and react to ideas, and (3) ask questions and figure things out. In short, they have fewer opportunities to *practice comprehension and logical thinking*.

So, we have work to do. We have to build background knowledge and give students frequent practice in explaining in order to strengthen their ability to comprehend.

DOGGIE BAG

1. Why is the Achievement Gap a *Literacy* Gap and in fact also an *Explanation* Gap?

2. What does the Comprehension Process entail, and how will you teach it to your students?

3. Why is background knowledge *so* important?

KEY CRITICAL READING SKILL 1: PARAPHRASING

You may be wondering why I have included the "four key critical *reading* skills" in the chapter on comprehension, when the next chapter is about reading. Although these four skills are reading skills, they are integral to the comprehension process, and they are also critical *thinking* skills. Take paraphrasing, for example. In combination with accessing background knowledge, it represents the first step toward understanding any "text," whatever that text might be. Because it is a thinking skill, it manifests itself in various forms of expression. Many of us paraphrase without even realizing that we are doing it—whether we're reading, writing, listening, speaking, smelling .... That's because we've had so much practice. But for many students—whether you call them beginning, struggling, "dependent,"[12] or "developing" readers[13]—paraphrasing is *not* automatic. And if you can't translate what you see, hear, smell, or otherwise sense into your own thoughts, you can't do much else with the text.

Reading both requires and enhances thinking. So when we work on our reading skills, we strengthen our thinking skills. Sadly, many students believe that good readers are simply born that way. They need to hear the message that reading involves a set of skills that they can practice and become good at. As you introduce different skills or strategies, you might say, "Here's another way to become a *strong* reader." Everyone wants to be strong. And PS: students need this training and reinforcement *at every level. We need to model the habits of effective readers not just with elementary students but also with middle and high school students.*

In order to be strong at paraphrasing, you must do the following:

1. **Unpack vocabulary.** In other words, use your word-attack skills and root knowledge to translate unfamiliar words. Of course, it also helps if you already know a lot of words.

2. **Unpack grammar and syntax.** One reason students struggle so mightily on the PSAT and SAT is that the passages tend to be constructed with long, complicated sentences. To decipher these difficult texts, students need to recognize transitions and signal words, and know how clauses and phrases function.

3. *Infer* **from idioms.** As strange and backwards as it sounds, you *do* have to infer in order to paraphrase. More on this oddity in a moment.

HOW CAN YOU TEACH STUDENTS HOW TO PARAPHRASE?

1. **Explain the Comprehension Process and how paraphrasing fits into it.** Like the rest of us, students need to know *what* they're supposed to be doing, and *why*. Also, it's easier to do something if you understand how it works. Comprehending, which we do *all the time*, involves a series of steps that can actually be taught. It's not magic. Everyone can become better at it. The same goes with paraphrasing. Who wouldn't want to learn these skills?

2. **Strengthen *their knowledge of roots.*** In every grade, we should provide direct instruction on vocabulary, with heavy doses of Latin and Greek roots, prefixes, and suffixes. While individual teachers can take this on, it also helps to have a schoolwide emphasis on vocabulary building. Some schools use the "Word of the Day" to boost vocabulary, but the words tend to be arbitrarily selected and unrelated to one another. Consequently, their meanings do not stick. I recommend trying the "Root of the Week" approach. Think of it this way: if you

learn a word, you only learn one word. If you learn a root, you could be learning a *dozen* words that use the same root.

With Root of the Week, the idea is that the target root is repeated *five times* in five different words throughout the week. The repetition reinforces the meaning of the root so that when students recognize it in different words, they are able to infer the meanings of words they haven't seen before. They build stronger root-attack and word-attack skills. They start to notice roots in the same way that people who have just bought a new car suddenly notice everyone else driving the same model. And they become more excited about words in general.

How can this approach work *schoolwide* (such as during morning announcements)? On Monday someone (ideally a student who has rehearsed with a teacher) introduces the Root of the Week and explains its meaning. Example: "cred," which means "believe." Then the presenter offers a word that uses that root, such as "credit," which is based on the belief that someone will pay you back. The presenter gives a user-friendly definition and synonyms, as well as a sentence using the word in context. On Tuesday, students are reminded of the same root and given a new word that uses the root (such as "incredible"). Then lather, rinse, repeat all week. Next week: different root. At University Heights Charter School in Newark, a turnaround school that saw dramatic gains in student achievement, the principal, Rahshene Davis, took this approach. She would introduce the Root of the Week and one word using the root each morning in Community Circle, then teachers followed up in their classrooms. Students who found the word in or outside of school somewhere or used it in context were given shout-outs the next morning in Community Circle. The school also featured the Root of the Week on a bulletin board in the main hallway, where parents could read it and discuss it with their children.[14]

See the TLC "Root of the Week" page for a sample PowerPoint for "cred."

Another approach is to use Root of the Week *in your individual classroom.* For the sake of efficiency, you can introduce all five words at one time and have students infer the meaning of the root according to how the words are used in context.

See the TLC "Root of the Week" page for a Sample Root of the Week Hypothesis Sheet for "cede/ceed"[15] and these Websites, which will make this idea easy to implement:

- http://www.learnthat.org/pages/view/roots.html (Possibly my favorite—very comprehensive!)

- https://www.msu.edu/~defores1/gre/roots/gre_rts_afx2.htm (General roots with words using them)
- http://readinglesson.com/pdffiles/bwdemo.pdf (includes a PDF file that you can download for free)
- http://www.macroevolution.net/root-word-dictionary.html#.UC50G44 voWlMvqpo (for science)
- http://dictionary.reference.com

3. **Teach *transitions* and *signal words*.** Sometimes it's not the big words that trip us up, it's the little ones. Students must be on the lookout for signal words that can help them decipher convoluted sentences. *Along with direct instruction on transitions and signal words, model your thought processes via think-aloud and read-aloud strategies.* (More on these in the During-Reading Strategies section in Chapter Two.)

It will also help students to *write* more effectively, knowing that it's their job to steer the reader with transitions. Students need to know what we mean by "logical flow." Don't assume that they know what "logical" means, so be prepared to offer some lessons on that. If you're frustrated with textbooks that define *transitions* merely as "time and order words," resulting in robotic writing that relies heavily on "first, second, and third," here are some Web pages (found on the TLC "Logic" page) that offer more nuanced explanations of what transitions are and how they work:

- http://www.virtualsalt.com/transits.htm
- https://www.msu.edu/~jdowell/135/transw.html
- http://www.studygs.net/wrtstr6.htm

One caveat: I've heard from teachers who said their students told them they'd "never heard of transitions" when they knew they had. It turned out that the previous teacher had called them "time and order" words. My suggestion is to teach students synonyms so that no matter what other people call them, they'll know what they are.

4. **Teach students how to use academic language effectively.** Check out Chapter Four, on speaking and listening, for a full explanation. In the meantime, here are two great books dealing with the use of academic language:

Graff, G., & Birkenstein, C. (2010). *They say/I say: The moves that matter in academic writing* (2nd ed.). New York: Norton.

Zwiers, J. (2008). *Building academic language: Essential practices for content classrooms.* San Francisco: Jossey-Bass.

5. **Teach *grammar* and *syntax*, especially *clauses* and *phrases*.** For many years, I wrestled with How to Teach Grammar. Should it stand alone, or somehow be incorporated into writing instruction? For students who couldn't pick a noun or a verb out of a lineup, where should I start? I experimented wildly. One of the most effective approaches involved a combination of direct instruction on types of clauses and phrases (with their accompanying punctuation) and writing conferences in which I said things like "I notice you've used an appositive here: what kind of punctuation do you need?" or "This doesn't look like a complete sentence yet. What's missing?" When students knew the terms and we could share this common language *for a purpose*, it was easier for them to remember *and use* the constructions. Their writing became more complex and, at the same time, clearer.

Students need to know Why Punctuation Is Important. In *Eats, Shoots, and Leaves*, Lynne Truss illustrates this point brilliantly with two letters that use exactly the same words but different punctuation. One is a love letter, the other a breakup letter. This example definitely catches the attention of teenagers: if you aren't careful with punctuation, you could intend to write someone a love letter and instead accidentally break up with him![16]

One of my favorite books on grammar instruction is *Mechanically Inclined*, by Jeff Anderson.[17] Unlike many people who waste countless hours forcing students to correct random errors (often without learning the rules), Anderson believes in showing models of *effective* grammatical constructs (such as beginning with two-word sentences) and having students imitate them. He posts anchor charts in his classroom and gives students opportunities to practice incorporating these elements in their writing. Harry Noden's *Image Grammar*[18] takes a similar exemplar-based approach, with a bit more emphasis on writing as an artistic enterprise.

6. **Teach students how to *infer meaning* from *idioms*.** Some people refer to paraphrasing as "literal comprehension," meaning "You can tell what is literally going on or being said." And to some extent, that's accurate. But there's more to it. In any given sentence, *figurative* things are also happening or being expressed, too.

On the road to comprehension, idioms are speed bumps. When we talk about reading comprehension gaps (to toss in another metaphor), I believe idioms are *the missing link.* No matter how you slice them (See? I can't help myself!), idioms are essential to lucid comprehension.

Look at this example: "Because my participation in the stock market had *cost me an arm and a leg*, I decided to invest in real estate instead."

The syntax in this sentence is somewhat complex and the vocabulary is somewhat challenging, but let's say you could break the clauses apart and find synonyms for "participation" and "invest." If you'd been listening to the news lately, "stock market" and "real estate" would not be unfamiliar terms, even if you didn't know much about them. You could probably paraphrase *most* of the sentence. But not the idiom. You'd have to *slow down* and *draw an inference about the idiom.* And while you might know the literal meanings of "cost," "me" "an arm" "and" and "a leg," you might not grasp what they meant when bundled together.

"How hard could it be?" you ask. I once sat in a seventh-grade classroom where students could not explain the expression "go out on a limb." And there was a tree visible through the window.

We assume that everyone knows these "simple" expressions. While the words in an idiom might be short, if you haven't ever heard a particular idiom, it's not so simple. And if English is not your first language, you are less likely to have heard common idioms. So when people use them, you don't understand what they're saying. And if they're telling a joke, you don't get it. That's frustrating. It can be tough on the joke teller, too. It took me several months of living with a Chinese roommate in grad school before I realized that it wasn't that she had no sense of humor; she just didn't comprehend most of my jokes.

Why don't our students know more about idioms? One problem is that English teachers often limit their discussion of figurative language to the context of poetry and fiction, emphasizing metaphors and similes only in those genres. Unless we point them out, students may fail to notice that idioms and other figurative uses of language also appear frequently in nonfiction—in newspapers and magazines and everyday conversation.

Here's the bottom line: students who struggle to speak standard English (whether English is their first language or not) will neither recognize nor comprehend standard English idioms. So we need to teach *both* the idioms *and* the strategies for figuring them out.

Here's a simple graphic organizer (found on the TLC "Idiom Power" page) that you can use as a Do Now to boost Idiom Power.

Here is the idiom.	Draw a picture of the idiom.	Paraphrase: What does it say, literally?	Draw an inference: What does this expression really mean? What's the message?
"A bird in the hand is worth two in the bush."		Having a bird in your hand is the equivalent of having two in a nearby hedge or tree.	It's better to have a little bit of something than to have none of it and only hope you can get more.
This homework was only "a drop in the bucket" compared to all of the work you'll be assigned this semester.			

These two Websites (which also appear on the TLC "Idiom Power" page) will help you teach idioms:

- http://www.idiomsite.com
- http://www.idiomconnection.com

7. **Train students *how to paraphrase strategically*.** Many students struggle with paraphrasing because they are unsure which words to *change* versus which to *keep*. They need a strategy for how to make these decisions.

Following is one that works, no matter what grade or subject you teach.

Step 1. *Circle* or *bracket* the words or phrases that you *cannot* or don't want to change. These words or phrases are crucial to the meaning of the passage and should not be changed because doing so would change that meaning. *Mnemonic hint: Help students remember what to circle by telling them to "wrap the words you want to keep in protective bubble wrap" and pretend to hug something precious.* The words you want to keep or "protect" might include:

- Proper nouns (unless they can be replaced by something that does not change their meaning, such as "Obama" → "the President")
- Statistics or specific information
- Words that are unique or difficult to find a synonym for

Step 2. *Underline* the words or phrases that you know you *can* change. Here are two examples:

Original	Paraphrased
A plan to start a [billion-dollar] government drug [development center] is a result of the Obama administration's concerns about the slowing pace of [new drugs] coming out of the [pharmaceutical] industry.[19]	An initiative to begin a billion-dollar national drug development center came about because the president and his colleagues are worried about how slowly new drugs are emerging from pharmaceutical companies.
[Two days] of talks between [Iran and six] world powers ended in failure [on Saturday, with Iran] refusing to engage on any concrete proposals to build confidence that [its nuclear program] is only for peaceful [purposes] and with no date set for another meeting.[20]	Two days of meetings involving Iran and six other nations ended unsuccessfully on Saturday because Iran refused to take any specific actions to prove that its nuclear program is not for military purposes, and there is no plan to meet again.

Note: Both of these statements were taken from *The New York Times*. Creating random sentences for practice presents an opportunity to review content or teach current events along the way. For handouts you can use with students to teach this strategy, see How to Paraphrase and How to Paraphrase: Third-Grade Practice on the TLC "Comprehension 101" page.

8. **After teaching the skill directly, weave paraphrasing practice into class discussions.** In addition to carrying content, class discussions provide opportunities to practice skills. An easy way to target paraphrasing is to ask students to "paraphrase or restate what was just said in your own words." I like to wink when I say it that way, to see who gets the joke. Another approach that works is during Think-Pair-Share: instead of asking students what *they* thought, ask them what their *partner* said.

9. **Make paraphrasing *fun*.** Last but not least, it's important to make paraphrasing enjoyable. One night while attending a performance of the Monty Python musical *Spamalot*, I realized (probably because I tend to see everything through comprehension-colored glasses) that it included some hilarious examples of paraphrasing. For instance, in the scene where King Arthur encounters Dennis the Peasant and explains how the Lady of the Lake made him king, Dennis mocks the absurdity of the concept by restating it in several different ways. This scene originally appeared in the movie *Monty Python and the Holy Grail*, and the clip can be seen on YouTube at http://www.youtube.com/watch?v=dOOTKA0aGI0

For more resources involving paraphrasing, check out the TLC "Comprehension 101" page and the TLC "Connecting Reading, Writing, and Test Prep" page.

DOGGIE BAG

1. What must you do in order to paraphrase well?
2. What role does paraphrasing play in the Comprehension Process?
3. How will you teach your students how to paraphrase strategically?
4. How can you weave more paraphrasing practice into your lessons?

KEY CRITICAL READING SKILL 2: INFERENCE

I am tempted to call this skill "Questioning and Inference" because in order to draw an inference you need to ask a question—usually Why? or How? In the comprehension process, you must also be able to paraphrase the text in order to draw a conclusion from it. This explains why analyses of critical reading assessment results often reveal that some students can paraphrase but cannot infer. Inference—which some call "extended reasoning"—is more rigorous.

Inference and explanation are two sides of the same coin. "Why did the man collapse?" You think about it and figure out, "He must have been sick." This is your inference, and you might explain further: "Most healthy people don't suddenly fall down."

Although inference is challenging, it can be practiced in many ways, and every form of practice will strengthen your students' comprehension skills. Each time you ask the question Why? and students have to explain their ideas, they are practicing inference. *If you maintain high standards for discourse in your classroom, requiring complete-sentence responses, you will boost not only fluency but also comprehension.* I agree wholeheartedly with Doug Lemov that "the complete sentence is the battering ram that knocks down the door to college."[21] I would also add, "And it's great low-hanging fruit for teachers who want to help students improve their reading and writing." The oral practice of expressing complete thoughts translates into more penetrating reading and more coherent writing, plus it teaches other students (who hear these complete explanations) more along the way. It's a win-win-win.

How does inference manifest itself in different content areas? Consider these similar tasks:

- Predict
- Extrapolate
- Hypothesize
- Deduce
- Solve
- Analyze
- Explain
- Surmise
- Figure out
- Make connections

When your students do any of these things, they are working on inference.

What I love most about inference is that it (1) engages students and (2) solidifies understanding. For instance, if a student asks, "What does X mean?" and I simply tell him a definition, he doesn't have to engage in any thinking, so he will either remember my definition or he will not. But if I use X in a sentence and he has to figure out the meaning for himself, he now *owns* the word.

Effective teachers don't simply sprinkle opportunities for inference into their lessons; instead, it drives their instruction. They view students not as containers or sponges, but as *sleuths*. I learned this firsthand from Charlie Speck, my high school Latin teacher, a truly brilliant man. Charlie was one of the reasons I became a teacher. He treated us as detectives and saw himself as the Chief Clue-Provider. He would string us along, dropping clue after clue, gradually leading us down the path until we understood even the most arcane Latin grammatical points. More than thirty years later, I still remember more about Latin than I do about World War I, which a handful of other teachers tried to teach me—most of them by slowly (and boringly, if that's a word) revealing facts on an overhead projector.

Students who are consistently asked to draw inferences tend to be more engaged and are less likely to become bored or disruptive. If you find yourself struggling with classroom management, study the techniques in Lemov's *Teach Like a Champion* and reflect on the extent to which your philosophy of teaching requires students to be sleuths. If students are fully engaged in learning—solving problems, figuring things out, and the like—then they are less likely to misbehave.

How Can You Teach Students How to Infer?

1. **Review the Comprehension Process and how inference works. Clarify the difference between paraphrasing and inference.** It is particularly important to point out the distinctions between paraphrasing and inference. Many students, especially those who might be labeled "concrete-sequential learners," can paraphrase but fail to grasp the concept of inference. They miss key ideas when reading and strain to explain their own ideas, particularly in writing.

This phenomenon became illuminated for me one day when I was trying to coach Isherra, a hard-working and enthusiastic student, in how to draw inferences. I had asked the class to pull three quotes from the latest chapter of *The Kite Runner*[22] by Khaled Hosseini and tell what they could infer from the quotes. Isherra, along with several others, had *paraphrased* her quotes.

As we sat together and I tried to explain what she needed to do, it occurred to me that she *knew* how to paraphrase and she *knew* how to infer, but she didn't know the *difference*. At that moment, the Falling Man was born. I created two posters, not just for Isherra—who said, "Ohhhhhhhhhhhhhh, I get it, Miss T!!!"—but for everyone else in the room who had missed this little mini-lesson. From that day forward, I could simply point to either poster, depending on what I was asking them to do.

Paraphrase	Inference
"The man fell down." → "He collapsed."	"The man fell down." → "He must have been sick."

I have since created a graphic organizer, cleverly titled the Paraphrasing and Inference Organizer, which looks like this:[23]

Original quote or passage	*Paraphrase* (then, in your head, ask "Why?" or "What can we infer?")	Draw an *inference* to answer "Why?"
My friend loves pizza.	My buddy adores pizza.	She probably likes cheese.

2. **Ask *why* as much as possible and require students to respond with complete sentences.** As discussed earlier, when students *explain* their ideas, they are employing their inference skills. Be sure to ask *why* even when students give you what you consider the "right" answer. Why? They might have merely guessed. Also, their explanation will teach others who might not have understood the issue or problem at hand.

I once asked a class, as a way of reviewing vocabulary, "Would you rather be described as *heinous*, or *grandiose*?" Javon, who rarely raised his hand, was practically launching himself out of his seat. So I called on him.

"Heinous," he said. "Definitely heinous."

Stifling a giggle (and the thought, *Are you kidding?*), I asked him why.

He looked me straight in the eye. "Because heinous is bad, but grandiose people think they're all that, and I wouldn't want someone to think of me that way."

The class erupted, "All right, Javon!!!" Meanwhile, I turned to the board quickly so that they wouldn't see the tears that had leapt to my eyes. In that moment, I realized several things: (1) I had underestimated him, (2) if I hadn't asked him why, I wouldn't have known how much he knew, and (3) he had just taught everyone else in the class both words in a context that they could understand. Asking *why* gives students a chance to explain what they know, and it gives them a chance to *shine*. Javon taught me that.

One caveat: If you have not been in the habit of asking students *Why?* they might react defensively or with less confidence. It's important to prepare them for this new approach so that they won't feel threatened and will instead take pride in their ability to explain their ideas.

3. **Make sure students understand the difference between *how* and *why*.** *How* and *why* can both elicit inferences and explanations, so they provide essential triggers for comprehension and expression. The problem is that although they seem like simple words, students often conflate them.

I figured this out one day while visiting a seventh-grade class that was revising responses to open-ended reading questions. I approached one girl who was chatting with her neighbor, evidently in an effort to avoid the assignment.

When I asked her how things were going, she replied bitterly, "My teacher gave me a 1 [out of 4], and I don't know why."

We began by looking at the Open-Ended Response Writing Rubric.[24] "Let's see if you restated the question," I suggested. The question was: "Explain how Sam's attitude toward the bird-calling contest changed throughout that day."

The girl had written, "Sam's attitude changed because . . ."

"Aha," I said. She stared at me quizzically. I told her, "I believe you know the answer to this question, but I think you approached it in slightly the wrong way. Let's see if I'm right, OK?"

She nodded.

"Let's pretend I walked into the classroom this morning wearing a parka, mittens, and a scarf. What could you infer about me, based on how I was dressed?"

"You were cold," she replied.

"Exactly. Now, say I took all of that apparel off by the end of class. *Why* would I make that change?"

"Because you were warm."

"Right. In this room, I would probably be sweating. Now, here's another question, and I want you to notice the difference: *How* would I have changed?"

"You would be wearing less clothing."

"Correct. Notice the difference between the *how* and *why* questions. Now, let's go back to your original question: *How* did Sam's attitude toward the bird-calling contest change throughout the day?"

"Oh," she said, and she was off to the races. Within a minute, she had explained *how*, and just for good measure, she also told me *why* his attitude had changed.

See, she understood the story. She just didn't understand the question.

4. **Require students to respond to *one another*, not just the teacher.** Why? For starters, they will learn more if they listen to one another. And again, they will gain more practice in explaining their ideas. *Note:* If you're having trouble getting students to listen to one another, check out *Teach Like a Champion*, especially Technique 32 (SLANT).[25]

5. **Avoid rhetorical questions.** "Julius Caesar wasn't really a great leader, was he?" or even "Was Julius Caesar really a great leader?" stated in a negative tone (and with a squinched-up face) makes the answer obvious. *Rhetorical questions are not really questions; therefore, they do not require students to think.* If you want to make an assertion, make one. Then ask a question that invites actual thought. Here are some examples:

- "I don't think Julius Caesar was a great leader. Why would I think that?" This approach requires students to empathize with you. Then you can follow up with, "Do you agree or disagree with me? Why?"

- "Some (uninformed) people think frogs are reptiles. Why would they think that?"

- Or make an assertion or an observation and ask, "Why is this true?" or "Why did this happen?" or "What caused this result or effect?" or "What do you think will happen next, and why?"

6. **Design assignments that require students to infer.** Check out the following snapshots of handy TLC graphic organizers:

Quotations to Paraphrasing and Inference[26]

Quotation	Paraphrase it	Draw an inference from it. (What does the speaker believe? What message is s/he trying to convey?)
"Change your thoughts and you change your world." Norman Vincent Peale	If you alter how you perceive things, it will alter how you experience life.	How we think affects how we behave.
"Nothing is worth more than this day." Johann Wolfgang von Goethe		

Character Traits: Quote and Explain[27]

Character Trait	Quote (evidence—include page numbers)	Explanation
Example: Stone Fox is *generous*.	"Stone Fox's dream was for his people to return to their homeland. Stone Fox was using the money he won from racing to simply buy the land back. He had already purchased four farms and over 200 acres" (p. 53).[28]	Stone Fox's people were kicked off of their land, and he enters dogsled races to use the winnings to support his people. His actions show that he cares deeply about his people.

Story Detectives[29]

Question	Answer (explanation)	Prove it! (evidence—include page numbers)
Example: How do the scoundrels fool people who work for the emperor? (based on "The Emperor's New Clothes" by Hans Christian Andersen[30])	The scoundrels say that if you can't see the clothing they design, you must be stupid or incompetent. The prime minister falls prey to this trick.	"I can't see anything," he thought (p. 2). "If I see nothing, that means I'm stupid! Or, worse, incompetent!" If the prime minister admitted that he didn't see anything, he would be discharged from his office.

Note: In the Story Detectives organizer, you can either provide the questions or ask your students to generate the questions. The key is that the questions must be open-ended (*how* or *why*) inference questions.

DOGGIE BAG

1. What is the difference between paraphrasing and inference?

2. What must one do in order to draw an inference?

3. How are inference and explanation two sides of the same coin?

4. How can you strengthen students' inference skills?

KEY CRITICAL READING SKILL 3: VOCABULARY IN CONTEXT (AND VOCABULARY INSTRUCTION)

The other day while listening to NPR on my way to work, it occurred to me that *party* means different things depending on what age you are. For kindergartners, it's all about the cupcakes. In college, maybe beer pong comes to mind. And if you're a forty-six-year-old woman who spends a lot of time commuting, you think of restaurants, Democrats, and Republicans. All of this is to say that when we teach vocabulary, maybe we should say, "Here's what it means now. But stay tuned!"

Figuring out word meanings based on the context, although an aspect of paraphrasing, deserves its own attention. We use this skill constantly, and it's often assessed separately on standardized tests—for example, via sentence completion questions on the PSAT and SAT. This skill also involves inference, because you have to draw an inference based on the context in order to figure out what a word means.

Vocabulary knowledge is vital to comprehension. So, how do we learn words? *By listening, by reading, and through instruction.*

Listening

Hart and Risley[31] found that if you hear lots of words, you will learn lots of words. It should also be clear that we are dependent on learning words orally until we learn how to read. But even after we learn to read, we continue to learn words by listening. My friend Rahshene Davis, formerly the principal at University Heights Charter School in Newark, likes to play this game with her son: she'll say a word, then he has to give a synonym, then she'll counter with another synonym, and so on until one of them runs out of vocabulary. For example, "Run"—"Dart"—"Jog"—"Dash"—"Sprint"—and so on.

She wasn't sure if this game was having an impact until one day (when he was ten years old) when she took him to Great Adventure with a friend. They were waiting in line at the Batman Ride, and her son commented to his buddy, "If I lived in Gotham City, I would totally *rely* on Batman."

His friend asked, "What does rely mean?"

Her son responded, "You know: depend on, count on . . ."

Bottom line: you can improve your students' vocabulary simply by speaking differently in class. Try this: "Who would like to help me *disseminate* these papers?" Or instead of saying, "Stop," try: "Halt, stop, cease, desist!" Students already know "stop." If you speak redundantly (paraphrasing and using synonyms . . .), they will infer the meanings of words they didn't previously know. Having to process the words by inferring their meaning will enable students to *own* the words. And they will start to *use* those words!

Reading

People like to say that we learn words from reading, and it's true. But how many words? Beck, McKeown, and Kucan report: "Studies estimate that of 100 unfamiliar words met in reading, between 5 and 15 of them will be learned (Nagy, Herman, & Anderson, 1985; Swanborn & de Glopper, 1999)."[32] That's not very encouraging.

The problem is that our ability to determine the meaning of an unfamiliar word depends on the context. Some contexts are helpful, while some actually hinder comprehension. Take this example:

> Sandra had won the dance contest, and the audience's cheers brought her to the stage for an encore. "Every step she takes is so perfect and graceful," Ginny said *grudgingly* as she watched Sandra dance.[33]

If you didn't know what "grudgingly" meant before you read this example, you might walk away thinking it had a positive connotation. Everyone else is admiring Sandra: why wouldn't Ginny? Beck, McKeown, and Kucan call this an example of "misdirective context" because the context is so misleading. On the other hand, this example also illustrates how we can help build vocabulary by reading aloud with proper expression and intonation. If you read it with feeling, students will grasp its counterintuitive meaning.

By contrast:

> When the cat pounced on the dog, he leapt up, yelping, and knocked down a shelf of books. The animals ran past Wendy, tripping her. She cried out and fell to the floor. As the noise and confusion mounted, Mother hollered upstairs, "What's all that *commotion?*"[34]

You would have to be tied up, blindfolded, and locked in a closet not to comprehend the meaning of *commotion* from all of the context clues. Beck, McKeown, and Kucan call this an example of "directive context" because it directs the reader to the meaning. I like to think of it as "instructive context" because the teacher purposefully creates sentences with enough context clues to suggest the meaning of the word being studied. Bottom line: that's the kind of context you should provide when introducing words to your students.

Instruction

My best advice for how to improve vocabulary instruction is to read *Bringing Words to Life*, by Isabel L. Beck, Margaret G. McKeown, and Linda Kucan.[35] Like many others who were taught a particular way and didn't know any better, before I read that book, I was guilty of giving students lists of words to define and write sentences for. Students would then create crazy sentences, and I would wonder what was wrong with them. Actually, nothing was wrong with *them*. They were simply doing what I'd asked them to do, which was crazy.

As Beck, McKeown, and Kucan point out, dictionaries suffer from many problems, not the least of which is lack of space. As a result, definitions are often too limited to be useful to someone trying to write a sentence with the word. My favorite example is this one:

> Disrupt: break up; split → "We disrupted the candy bar so we could all share it."[36]

This definition of *disrupt* isn't bad, but it's inadequate. And if you look at the sentence, it makes some sense, given the lame definition: the student has applied her background knowledge of candy bars and friendship to use the new word in a context she's familiar with. While you're busy asking, "What were you thinking???" she's feeling proud of herself for demonstrating the positive character trait of sharing.

Effective vocabulary instruction has three phases: (1) select and introduce, (2) review and reinforce, and (3) assess.

Select and Introduce

Beck, McKeown, and Kucan recommend selecting "Tier 2" words.[37] Following is a quick primer on their three tiers of vocabulary.

Tier 1	Tier 2	Tier 3
Basic words that typically do not require instruction	*High-frequency* words for mature language users; found across a *variety* of domains	*Low-frequency* words often limited to specific domains; *jargon*; arcane or archaic words
dog, talk, sad	robust, absurd, marinate	parallelogram, neutron, alliteration

When trying to decide if a word belongs in Tier 2, ask yourself the following questions:

- Is it important and useful? (Do most educated adults know this word?)
- Can it be used in multiple contexts? (Think *revolution*.)
- Do students already understand the general concept of this word? (For example, *robust* is a synonym for *strong*, a concept they should already know.)

To introduce new words, here are the key steps:

- Provide the words in sentences that offer *instructive or directive* context.
- Explain meanings in user-friendly language and elaborate.
- Teach pronunciation. If students can't say the word, they won't use it in speech *or* writing. I highly recommend choral practice in which you pronounce the word, then point to the class and say the word with them, repeated at least three times.
- Teach differences, contexts, and nuances.

I like to use the following simple format for introducing the words.

Word [with space to write more information about the word]	*Sentence using word:* circle the context clues.	*Speculation:* **What do you think this word means, judging by context clues?**
disrupt	A power outage that left us in the dark <u>disrupted</u> our meeting until someone located the candles.	[Students record their ideas about what they think the word means.]

Review and Reinforce

Once students have had some initial exposure to the words, you'll need to review and reinforce meanings in various ways. Here are some suggestions:

- **Teach pronunciation.** Students who can't pronounce the words won't use them, either orally or in writing. If they can't sound them out, they won't write them. My favorite tactic is to establish a routine where I pronounce the word then open my hands toward the class and pronounce it with them, repeating this three times to ensure I've engaged any potential stragglers. I do this *any* time a student struggles with pronunciation because I know that if one student can't pronounce a word, then others probably can't, either. This "choral pronunciation" approach spares struggling individuals any embarrassment and sends a message to the entire class that "we are all in this together, all learning together."

- **Post the words for easy reference.** In my travels, I've seen many different forms of Word Wall organization (such as alphabetical, parts of speech, or synonyms and antonyms), but I'm not sure that there is one best approach. My friend Katy Wischow, a fabulous middle school English teacher at Greater Newark Charter School, notes that Word Walls get more use when you play games with them (like, "Who can find two synonyms on the wall?" or, "Which words have to do with _____ concept?" which allows for explanation, or, "Which words have a negative connotation?"[38] You can design endless variations. As long as students *use* the words, that's all that matters. And on that point, it's helpful to praise those who do.

- **Use the words as much as possible yourself.** Consider challenging the class: "Let's see which one of us can use more Word Wall words this period!" Also, share your vocabulary lists with colleagues so that they can reinforce the words, too.

- **Give students frequent opportunities to engage in wordplay.** Beck, McKeown, and Kucan[39] offer numerous suggestions (such as the one mentioned earlier: "Would you rather be described as _____, or _____?"), and I won't repeat them. You should buy their book.

- **Play games with the words.** Jessica Majerus, an excellent middle school English teacher at North Star Academy Charter School in Newark, developed an engaging vocabulary review game-activity that takes only three minutes. Students earn points for creating sentences using the vocabulary words. After they create their sentence, they pass a ball to someone else in the room. She tracks the "class points" on a clipboard and assigns them as follows:
  - 1 point = attempt
  - 2 points = correct usage
  - 3 points = context makes the meaning of the word clear

In her description of the game, which is available on the TLC "Building Robust Vocabulary" page, she notes: "You need to hear a new word seven times to learn it. By playing this game, students get to hear the words being used over and over. They are  practicing just by listening. I can easily assess misconceptions or usage errors and correct them as we play the game or address them later. The class has to work together. The game goes by quickly, and if they argue or yell for the ball, they don't earn the points."[40]

- **Make it cool.** Encourage students to use "strong" vocabulary. Everyone wants to be strong. At Soaring Heights Charter School in Jersey City, teachers created a bulletin board with headshots of students glued to drawings of muscular bodies holding up their favorite strong vocabulary words.

Assess

The most important thing to remember about vocabulary assessment is that students must demonstrate that they can *use* the words. That is why matching words to definitions is not sufficient. Following are some alternative types of questions to consider (which Jessica Majerus developed[41] based on her reading of *Bringing Words to Life*).

Answer the question. Use your knowledge of our vocabulary to answer the following questions (two points each).

Which of these do you think should be *compulsory*: buckling your seatbelt in a car or being in your house by 8:00 pm? Why?

_____

_____

_____

_____

Scenarios. Pick the scenario that best matches the word and defend your answer (two points each).

Word	Scenario 1	Scenario 2
interspersed	I was so angry that my writing was mixed with invectives.	I was so angry that my writing was made up completely of invectives.

....

Why?

_____

_____

_____

_____

Using stronger words in writing. Improve the paragraph below by crossing out the weak word(s) and replacing each with a stronger word. Write the stronger word above the crossed-out word. Make sure to use the correct form of the word. I am looking for <u>four vocabulary words</u> to be used, but if you see other opportunities to use stronger vocabulary, I will give you extra credit for doing so (two points each).

In *Night*,[42] Elie was very scared when he went to Auschwitz. When he arrived there was a big commotion, but then the guards forced all of the prisoners to line up and have their heads shaved. After this, they were told to strip and were given prison clothes to wear. It was a joke though, because they were given the wrong size clothes to wear. They were then looked at to see if they were strong enough. Of course, the guards treated them badly and yelled and cursed at them. These experiences, and seeing the crematorium, made Elie lose faith that God would rescue his people from the evil of the Nazis.

Using context clues. Read the passages to figure out which definition is best for the italicized word (three points each).

- 1 point = underlining context clues that make sense (underlining the whole passage doesn't count)
- 1 point = explaining your choice with reasons (even if you get the wrong answer, if your thinking is logical and clear, you can earn this point)
- 1 point = picking the correct answer

Which of these most closely matches the meaning of *stocky* in the passage below?

"He was a *stocky* man with big shoulders, the neck of a bull, thick lips, and curly hair" (p. 47).

a. sturdy

b. thin

c. mean

d. angry

Why?

_____

_____

_____

_____

_____

_____

DOGGIE BAG

1. How do we learn words?

2. What are Tier 2 vocabulary words?

3. What strategies will you use to teach vocabulary more effectively?

KEY CRITICAL READING SKILL 4: INFERRING MAIN IDEA OR ARGUMENT (AKA SUMMARIZING)

We now arrive at the critical reading skill that students often struggle with the most.

For decades, possibly centuries, teachers and standardized tests have exhorted students to "find the main idea." They search and search, and they just can't find it. Although it's true that the thesis of a nonfiction piece is often located in the first paragraph, and subsequent paragraphs should have topic sentences that one can identify, "find" is an inexact word for what readers actually must do. It's not a Where's Waldo? exercise. And in the case of fiction, there are no thesis statements or topic sentences to point to. More often than not, no matter what you read, finding the main idea is more accurately described as an act of *inference*.

How Can You Teach Students How to Infer the Main Idea or Argument (AKA Summarize)?

1. **Review the Comprehension Process and explain how we accumulate inferences as we work through a text to arrive at the main idea or argument.** Make sure students know what inference is and how the accumulation of inferences and insights in any given text adds up to a main idea or argument. Model how you do this in both nonfiction and fiction so that students can see the similarities and differences. PS: Don't forget that this approach applies to *any* "text": portraits, political cartoons, song lyrics, geometric proofs, scientific theories, and so forth.

2. **Clarify what we mean by *main idea*.** Unfortunately, the word *idea*, which is clean and beautiful when you have a good one, turns muddy when overused. Far

too many people conflate *idea* with *topic*. This explains why students often give one-word answers such as "Running" or "Terrorism" when asked for the main idea. "Running, though challenging, can be good for your health" is a legitimate main idea. Or more precisely, it's a main *argument*. One of my goals in life is to convince everyone I meet to stop using *main idea* and switch to—or at least include—*main argument*. Maybe I'm naïve, but I think a small change in word choice could make a big difference in comprehension.

So, Step 2 is to clarify that you want to know what the main *argument* is, and it should be expressed as a *complete sentence*. Giving students examples is a fine way to illustrate this idea—er, argument. It is also important to note that pieces of fiction and narrative writing don't have arguments; they have *themes* or messages. Following is a handy poster.

What is the *main idea*?

- In nonfiction: *main argument*
- In fiction or narrative: *message, lesson, theme*

---

3. **Teach the difference between *argument* and *evidence*.** Not long after your first attempt to elicit main arguments from students, you will undoubtedly notice that they often conflate *argument* and *evidence*. Also, if you've been reading the Common Core Standards, you're aware of their emphasis on the use of evidence to make arguments. (PS: For more information on the Common Core State Standards, see http://www.corestandards.org. Also, check out the TLC "Standards" page for the K–12 ELA Common Core Standards Tracking Sheet, which lists each grade's standards in a separate spreadsheet. A snippet of this document, which is particularly handy when writing or evaluating curriculum, appears in the Appendix of this book.) So, Step 3 is to teach students how to recognize the difference between the two. I recommend this simple approach: give them a list of sentences about whatever content you're dealing with at the moment. Some of those sentences should be facts (that is, evidence), some arguments (that is, claims, opinions, or debatable statements), and they all require proof or evidence for support. Following are a few examples.[43]

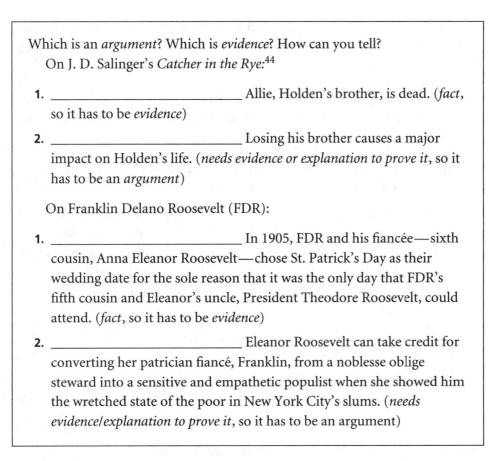

Which is an *argument*? Which is *evidence*? How can you tell?

On J. D. Salinger's *Catcher in the Rye*:[44]

1. _____ Allie, Holden's brother, is dead. (*fact, so it has to be evidence*)

2. _____ Losing his brother causes a major impact on Holden's life. (*needs evidence or explanation to prove it*, so it has to be an *argument*)

On Franklin Delano Roosevelt (FDR):

1. _____ In 1905, FDR and his fiancée—sixth cousin, Anna Eleanor Roosevelt—chose St. Patrick's Day as their wedding date for the sole reason that it was the only day that FDR's fifth cousin and Eleanor's uncle, President Theodore Roosevelt, could attend. (*fact, so it has to be evidence*)

2. _____ Eleanor Roosevelt can take credit for converting her patrician fiancé, Franklin, from a noblesse oblige steward into a sensitive and empathetic populist when she showed him the wretched state of the poor in New York City's slums. (*needs evidence/explanation to prove it*, so it has to be an argument)

See the TLC "Connecting Reading, Writing, and Test Prep" page for more exemplars. We will revisit argument versus evidence further in Chapter Three, in the section on What Students Struggle With the Most When They Write.

In the process of teaching argument and evidence, you might want to try what my friend Katy Wischow calls the "Boxes and Bullets" approach. Students put the argument sentence in a box, then list bulleted details that support the argument right below it. You can also train students to do this during read-alouds; they orally or mentally say the main idea and point to their hand, then tick off supports on their fingers.[45] Whether they draw the boxes and bullets or point to their hands and fingers, this approach helps students visualize the difference between arguments and evidence.

4. **Teach students how to recognize *topic sentences*.** Once students have a clearer sense what an argument is (not the kind that involves flinging plates or

profanity), it will be easier for them to recognize topic sentences. Even so, no one emerges from the womb knowing how to find a topic sentence. So, some training is in order. Try this next approach.

Give students a paragraph (ideally with content relevant to something longer that they are about to read, to provide background knowledge) and model the following:

1. When looking for the topic sentence in a paragraph, we want to narrow our search down to the first few sentences.

2. Look for a sentence that raises *How?* or *Why?* questions. Also look for "debatable or arguable" words. Adjectives tend to be debatable. For example, what is *your* definition of *exciting*? It's probably different from that of the person sitting next to you. So if you wanted to make an argument about something being "exciting," you'd need to provide evidence and explanation.

3. Test that sentence by creating a How? or Why? question that mentions the topic.

4. Look in the paragraph for evidence or proof that answers the question, and if you can find that evidence, you have correctly identified the topic sentence.

Here's an example I drafted about the desk of a typical fifth-grader:

It's true. The inside of a typical fifth-grader's desk is difficult to keep organized and clean. There is never enough room for all of the textbooks, workbooks, independent reading books, binders, and notebooks, much less the pens, pencils, and erasers. Plus, because students are normally not permitted to leave their seats during class, it is tempting to use the desk as a personal trash can. Crumpled paper, used tissues, bent paper clips, and loose pencil shavings need a place to go, and the desk makes a convenient hiding spot.

Explanation

- Sentence 1 is transitional and too vague to be an argument.
- Sentence 2 raises this question: "*Why* is the inside of a typical fifth-grader's desk difficult to keep organized and clean?" The word *difficult* is debatable or

arguable (because we all define *difficult* differently), so it establishes an argument that warrants evidence and explanation.

- Sentence 3 begins to answer the question raised in Sentence 2. The rest of the paragraph provides the evidence and explanation to support the argument in Sentence 2.

Therefore, this is the topic sentence: *The inside of a typical fifth-grader's desk is difficult to keep organized and clean.*

Note: We will revisit topic sentences in Chapter Three, in the section on What Students Struggle With the Most When They Write.

5. **Give students frequent opportunities to *summarize*.** Start small. Don't hand out copies of Homer's *Iliad*[46] and ask for a summary. One approach is to ask students to read an untitled passage and give it a title. Another effective technique is to give students quotations relevant to your current content so that they can practice one sentence at a time while simultaneously reviewing relevant subject matter. Shrinking a sentence is a form of summarizing.

"Wait a minute," I can hear someone saying. "Isn't that paraphrasing?"

Yes, and it is also summarizing because you are limiting the restatement to the Most Important Information. Think of *paraphrasing as retelling*, and *summarizing as highlighting*. Summarizing a quote makes a great Do Now, and when you appeal to students' competitive spirit, it increases engagement. The following example explains how.

See if you can condense the following sentence to ten words or fewer:

- "It is easy in the world to live after the world's opinion; it is easy in solitude to live after our own; but the great man is he who in the midst of the crowd keeps with perfect sweetness the independence of solitude." (Ralph Waldo Emerson, from "Self-Reliance"[47])

Think of summarizing as weightlifting. You don't start by trying to bench-press 250 pounds. Begin instead with numerous light repetitions and build your way up to longer, more complex texts.

6. **Teach students how to figure out what's important.** Not long after our students did poorly on "main idea" questions on an interim assessment, several colleagues and I sat down and tried to figure out what we could do. The story of what we decided appears in Chapter Two, in the section on Nonfiction Versus Everything Else. It includes the What's Important Organizer, which also appears on the TLC "Analyzing Literature" page.

DOGGIE BAG

1. What is the "main idea" in nonfiction? What is the "main idea" in fiction?
2. Why do your students need to know the difference between argument and evidence, and how will you teach this?
3. How will you teach your students to find topic sentences?
4. What strategies will you use to strengthen your students' ability to infer the main idea or argument?

TLC DOWNLOAD ZONE FOR COMPREHENSION PROCESS

Sample PowerPoint for "cred"

Sample Root of the Week Hypothesis Sheet for "cede/ceed"

How to Paraphrase

How to Paraphrase: Third-Grade Practice

Paraphrasing and Inference Organizer

Open-Ended Response Writing Rubric

Quotations to Paraphrasing and Inference

Character Traits: Quote and Explain

Story Detectives

K–12 ELA Common Core Standards Tracking Sheet

What's Important Organizer

Reading

DECODING + FLUENCY AND COMPREHENSION = READING

As our discussion of comprehension should have made plain, reading is not like making Kool-Aid: you can't just add water and stir. Some people think decoding alone is reading. I've heard teachers say, "They can read the words on the page, but they have no idea what they're saying." *If students do not comprehend, they're not fully reading yet*.

Our job as teachers is twofold: (1) explain to parents what we mean by "reading" and how they can help, and (2) teach students how to read. Of course, this sounds much simpler than it is.

Regarding Job 1, I highly recommend Jim Trelease's *Read-Aloud Handbook*, which makes a compelling case for why parents *must* read to their children and how it will boost their academic performance. He notes that in reading aloud, we accomplish the following: "condition the child's brain to associate reading with pleasure; create background knowledge; build vocabulary; provide a reading role model."[1] Moreover, as Trelease points out, "Nobody has a favorite vowel or a favorite blend. What motivates children and adults to read more is that (1) they like the experience a lot, (2) they like the subject matter a lot, and (3) they like and follow the lead of people who read a lot."[2] Parents need to understand how vital their role is in this regard: what a huge impact it can make—and how easy it is, really—to read aloud to their children. Presenting a parent workshop based on Trelease's book would be a great way to build enthusiasm at the beginning of the school year. In subsequent years, parents could stand up and give testimonials to encourage their peers.

Now for Job 2: if your students cannot sound out words, you have to start there, with decoding and phonics instruction. This book is not a phonics primer.

Kylene Beers provides a useful introduction to the world of phonics.[3] Here are two helpful Websites for teachers *and* parents:

- Starfall describes itself as "a free public service to teach children to read with phonics." It provides various activities for child-directed instruction. (http://www.starfall.com)
- MeeGenius "features beautifully illustrated and engaging e-books with Read-Along Technology, so that budding readers develop word recognition by seeing words while hearing them pronounced." It offers free and low-cost access to classic children's literature. (http://www.meegenius.com)

My main point in bringing up decoding is that we need to keep our eyes on the ball: we need to make sure *all* of our students are reading on grade level, and if they're not, we need to help them get there. I've been in too many schools where their policy of social promotion enables the adults to shirk this responsibility. In many failing schools and districts, students enter kindergarten unable to read—and then are not taught to read well enough to catch up. Parents don't want their kids to fail. And, of course, kids don't want to be held back. But when they reach third grade and can't read the standardized tests, they won't pass those tests. And so it will continue in fourth grade, fifth grade, and onward. If they keep getting promoted, they might make it to high school. But they won't graduate. I don't know why anyone is *surprised* at the high dropout rates in some districts. When you think about it, if you were in ninth grade and could barely read, you'd feel angry, frustrated, and depressed, too. In this situation, faced with the prospect of several more years of failure, dropping out would seem like a logical decision.

So—we have work to do.

About fluency, Lemov asserts that it "consists of automaticity plus expression plus comprehension,"[4] and I agree. In order to read expressively, you have to understand what you're reading. Modeling dramatic reading for students will help. Giving them practice will also help. Partner reading can make this process more efficient, and you can reconvene the whole class to share highlights and reinforce key points: "Who wants to read the part where . . . ?" It's important to have fair expectations of students who, unlike you, are not reading Hamlet's soliloquy for the four-hundredth time. No matter how students perform, you can always find a way to put a positive spin on it. As Lemov notes, if someone delivers a performance that is too wooden, you can respond: "OK, now that you've got the words, let's go back and read it with energy. This is an exciting part of the book!" And if the reading was done well, it wouldn't hurt to repeat it: "Oh, that was great! Can you read it again so we can all hear how surly you made it sound?"[5]

In Chapter One, we addressed the comprehension process and the four key critical reading skills. Beyond providing students with a basic understanding of comprehension and the required skills, we must also train them in how to read *strategically*. More on this in a moment. First, a commercial interruption for nonfiction.

NONFICTION VERSUS EVERYTHING ELSE

Label the following genres as NF (nonfiction) or F (fiction). Even if you think some could be *both*, pick the one that is *mostly* true.

Novels	F
Newspaper articles	
Math textbook passages	
Science textbook passages	
Social studies textbook passages	
Informational text on state assessments	
Narrative passages on state assessments	
Magazine articles	
Wikipedia entries	
Letters to the editor	
Editorials	
Directions for appliances	
Credit card bills	
Research studies	
The scroll on CNN and other news channels	
Most of the passages on the PSAT, SAT, and GRE	

Then turn the page.

What did you notice? Yep, virtually all are nonfiction except the one already labeled F. Narrative passages on tests could be fiction, but they are often *personal* narratives—that is, nonfiction. Anything else? Well, we *hope* news scrolls are nonfiction. But sometimes you wonder.

The point here should be obvious: most of the reading we do in the real world is nonfiction. Yet in language arts classes, where teachers are most directly responsible for teaching reading, students have traditionally read mostly stories, plays, or poems. Not nonfiction.

Recently, the Common Core State Standards (which most states have adopted) have proposed to address this problem by putting more emphasis on nonfiction. (PS: For more information on the Common Core State Standards, see http://www.corestandards.org. Also, check out the TLC "Standards" page for the K–12 ELA Common Core Standards Tracking Sheet, which lists each grade's standards in a separate spreadsheet. A snippet of this document, which is particularly handy when writing or evaluating curriculum, appears in the Appendix of this book.)

For me, the problem became apparent even before the Common Core came to town. One day, as several colleagues and I analyzed the results of a ninth-grade critical reading assessment, we noticed that students had done poorly on "inferring main idea," and we were trying to figure out how to reteach this skill.

"How do you teach main idea when you're reading a novel?" someone said.

"Read more nonfiction," someone else responded. We laughed, but it was true. We began to revise the curriculum. In every subject, we set out to identify more short nonfiction passages that would provide background knowledge leading up to the reading of other texts. We also designed projects that put more emphasis on nonfiction, such as the Nonfiction Book Talk Project, the DBQ Approach, and the Research Paper. (PS: These are all described in detail in later chapters.)

We also recognized that we couldn't completely abandon fiction, so we had to teach students how to figure out what was important when reading literature. At first, I tried simply asking them to "list the five most important things in Chapter Six," but when Terrell raised his hand and said, "Miss Tantillo, how are we supposed to know what's important?" I realized that although experienced readers have a heuristic for determining what is important when reading fiction, many students do not. So I invented the What's Important Organizer, which appears next and on the TLC "Analyzing Literature" page, along with a completed model.

Name _____ Date _____

What's Important Organizer[6]: Chapter #_____

Directions: Use *complete sentences* to answer all five questions. You may either *paraphrase* or *provide quotes* to support your assertions, but either way, you *must give page numbers* to indicate where the evidence can be found. Refer to the model to ensure that you are doing this properly. Give *at least two pieces of evidence per question.*

1. *Decisions with purpose:* What major decisions do the characters make, and why?

   _____

   _____

   _____

2. *Conflicts, obstacles, or challenges:* What conflicts, obstacles, or challenges do the characters face, and how do they deal with them?

   _____

   _____

   _____

3. *Lessons, insights, or messages:* What lessons do any of the characters learn? What do *we* learn?

   _____

   _____

   _____

4. *Causes and effects:* What events or actions have major effects on characters? How do the characters react?

   _____

   _____

   _____

5. *Patterns:* What patterns from either this passage or the rest of the book do you notice in this passage?

   _____

   _____

   _____

DOGGIE BAG

1. Why is it necessary for students to read lots of nonfiction?

2. How can you teach "main idea" when reading fiction?

DIFFERENT TYPES OF READERS

Growing up, I sat in many classrooms that were divided into rows. This arrangement didn't lend itself to partner work or group work, and I suspect it also led some teachers to view us as a homogeneous clump—to believe that we all processed information in similar ways and had equivalent reading and writing experiences and skills. When I became a teacher myself, I realized that such assumptions were incorrect. I needed to address students' different learning styles, experiences, and skills in order to help them reach their fullest potential.

One place to start when considering how to differentiate instruction is to focus on the needs of different types of readers. Although students of the same age may have had similar life experiences, their reading experiences may be vastly divergent.

In *The Book Whisperer*, Donalyn Miller describes three different readers. First, *developing* readers—or as she notes, what most people call *struggling* readers: these are students not reading on grade level.[7] Kylene Beers refers to this group as "dependent," which is also accurate, but for the moment let's go with Miller's more optimistic spin.[8] While some may have learning disabilities, it is also possible that they simply have not had enough exposure to reading and that with more practice they could improve dramatically. Miller's major thesis is that in order to become a stronger reader, you have to read. It may sound obvious, but many developing readers find themselves in remedial classes where the work involves exercises focused on skills, not actual reading. As their peers gain more practice in reading and are exposed to more content, which builds their background knowledge to make them stronger readers, the developing readers fall further behind, and the achievement gap widens.

The second type Miller describes is the *dormant* reader. These students do their homework and pass the tests but don't read for fun. They see reading as work, not pleasure. The problem is that they don't even realize they have a problem. But, as Miller rightly notes, students in this cohort "run the risk of falling behind students who read more than they do."[9] To address the needs of these students, we must find ways to help them fall in love with reading. Miller recommends providing more opportunities for independent reading. More on this in a moment.

The third type, the *underground* readers, are avid readers who "see the reading they are asked to do in school as completely disconnected from the reading they prefer to do on their own."[10] They read their own books secretly during class discussions and resent the slow pace of whole-class reading. In classes where students do not have the freedom to choose books or read independently, these students become bored and frustrated. We need to provide some options for them so that they can become more invested in the class; we need to honor their love of reading and push them to higher levels of rigor and sophistication. We also need to channel their passion for reading toward texts and genres that they might not have chosen on their own to expand their intellectual horizons and strengthen their academic muscles.

My friend Rahshene Davis, who was the principal at University Heights Charter School in Newark and co-led a turnaround that resulted in dramatic gains in student achievement, decided that she preferred to start with positive language. She encouraged her teachers to categorize children by the *level of support* they needed instead of their ability. As she pointed out to me, "Terms like 'struggling, low, and at-risk' name their ability, and ability is not as fluid as 'level of support.'" She and her teachers used the terms *high support* and *low support*. Students who needed more support from the teacher in a particular skill or strategy would be referred to as *high support*, and students who were strong in a skill or strategy and needed less support from the teacher would be *low support*. Once students obtained and mastered the skill or strategy, they could move to low support.[11]

Whatever you call the different types of readers in your school, you've got to identify them *quickly*, provide appropriate support, and monitor their progress. The next few sections focus on how to customize that support and teach strategies that strengthen students' comprehension skills.

DOGGIE BAG

1. What are the different types of readers?

2. Which type were you in elementary, middle, or high school?

3. Can you identify the different types of readers in your classes?

INDEPENDENT AND GUIDED READING

When I taught high school English, I was very aware of my responsibility to prepare my students for college. Although I'd been an underground reader myself, I'd also been careful to play the game so that I could earn good grades and go to a solid university. Like every other college student, I soon found that while we could choose our own courses, we were forced to read whatever the professors assigned. So when I started teaching, it didn't occur to me to give students many choices: I designed the curriculum explicitly to train them for the kind of work they'd have to do in college. They needed to analyze challenging texts and build their reading stamina. In short, my general attitude was this: you can read any book you want as long as it's one that I've chosen.

Whenever I distributed a new book, a handful of students would whine, "Oh, no, not another one! Why do we have to read *this* book?" I didn't take it personally; these were typically students who didn't like to read, and they said the same thing every time. I did my best to hook them, and usually within a week or two, they were admitting how much they loved the book.

Nevertheless, their complaints didn't fall on completely deaf ears. As the years wore on, I found ways to include more opportunities for students to choose their own books: through independent reading, research papers, and Book Talk Projects.

Students take more ownership of their learning when they have some say in deciding what it entails. But on the high school level, because they need to be ready to read what's on their college syllabi, we cannot simply let them read whatever they feel like. When their peers in college mention *Romeo and Juliet*,[12] for example, we don't want them to say, "Romeo and who?" They need exposure to commonly read high school texts. Therefore, when designing curriculum, we must find a balance between assigned and freely chosen texts.

Working with K–8 teachers in the past five years, I've come to see reading instruction from a slightly different perspective. The priorities in K–8 differ from those in high school. In K–8, you have to teach children how to read and help them fall in love with reading. It's important to share some common texts—to provide mini-lessons focused on important skills and strategies, to use passages on grade level with proper scaffolding, to build a sense of community and culture around shared texts, and to deepen their collective knowledge base. But it's also important to provide more differentiated opportunities to meet the needs of different readers in your room.

By implementing a system of guided reading, especially in K–5 or so, you can assess students' reading levels with accuracy, match them with leveled texts, and provide targeted small-group instruction. Fountas and Pinnell (among others) have written entire books on guided reading,[13] so I will not repeat the details. Suffice it to say that it's an approach worth pursuing. When students have access to books on their "just right" reading level (books that don't totally frustrate them), they are more inclined to read.

Because K–8 schedules tend to prioritize literacy instruction—such as through self-contained classes, block periods, and interdisciplinary instruction—they offer more opportunities for reading practice, including more time for independent reading. Many schools have tried Drop Everything And Read (DEAR), with varying degrees of success. DEAR is like anything else: it can work well if you implement it effectively—if not, then not. DEAR doesn't work when students don't have appropriate books to read, when the books are not on their level, or not engaging, or both. So they fake-read or behave disruptively. It's painful to watch. But it doesn't have to be this way! Donalyn Miller helps her students select books on their independent-reading level that they will love, acting like a personal librarian for each student.[14] One of Miller's most startling findings is that giving students time to read in class in fact increases the amount of reading they do at home. As one of her students reported: "Reading in class makes me read more at home and on the weekends because if I am caught in a book, *I have to finish it.*"[15] The results are astounding. Most of her students read more than forty books per year and, not surprisingly, do very well on standardized tests.

DOGGIE BAG

1. How much independent reading do your students do? Why?
2. If you don't currently implement a guided reading program, would it help your students to try it?

INTRODUCTION TO READING STRATEGICALLY

While I appreciate Miller's positive framing of "developing" readers, the framework that Beers presents, of "independent versus dependent" readers, is also instructive. Dependent readers "depend on an outside-of-themselves source not only to tell them what to do but in many cases, to do it for them."[16] They need support and aren't sure what to do when they don't understand a text; often they skip parts they don't understand or cross their arms and give up.

Many students fail to realize that good readers read *strategically*. Or, as one of Beers's students remarked: "This is really hard work. You do this all the time?"[17] Part of our job as teachers—no matter what grade or subject we teach—is to convey the different strategies that good readers use. Students need to learn strategies that they can apply not just to the text at hand but also to the next one, and the next one, and so on. Having these tools in our toolbox gives us more confidence that we are prepared for the challenges that will arise. If we have multiple tools, we can avoid acting like the man with a hammer, who sees everything as a nail. The key is not just to *have* the tools, but to know precisely when and how to use them.

BEFORE-READING STRATEGIES

Preparing to read a text is a bit like preparing to dive into the ocean. Whether you've done it before or not, you shouldn't simply sprint forward with your eyes closed and jump in. You could be in for a sudden freeze or a broken neck. If you know anything about the ocean, you approach it with both enthusiasm and respect. You decide whether you want to float around or ride your surfboard. You check the waves and tide, note whether anyone in the water is drifting or being pulled by the current, and wade in to acclimate yourself to the temperature. If you're an experienced swimmer, you'll probably take these steps almost without thinking and soon find yourself floating peacefully or eagerly catching waves.

Along these same lines, good readers spend some time checking out the text before they dive into it. They approach it with a sense of purpose. They reflect on previous experiences related to the text. They develop questions and make predictions. Probably the most important thing they do, given how the comprehension process works, is make connections with their prior knowledge[18] or as Keene and Zimmerman refer to it, activate their "schema."[19] The amount of background knowledge we bring to a text  directly correlates to how well we will comprehend it. It's vital for students to use what they already know as they approach a text. As Beers notes, "The more we frontload students' knowledge of a text and help them become actively involved in constructing meaning prior to reading, the more engaged they are likely to be as they read the text."[20] Unfortunately, sometimes students don't realize that they *should* access prior knowledge, like the girls in one class I observed who didn't grasp that their experiences as Brownies would have helped them understand a story that mentioned Brownies until their teacher pointed this out.

Even students who know they should use prior knowledge sometimes fail to realize that they *have* any—especially if it comes from a different class or subject. We need to train them to keep their minds open to this possibility. As Cris Tovani notes, "Teachers have an important role helping students acquire new knowledge. However, their job is easier if they first teach students how to use information they already know."[21] Here is an argument for more interdisciplinary teaching: so that students will use *everything* they know when reading (and writing).

Of course, if students have *zero* background knowledge regarding a text you're planning to introduce, you'll need to provide some. When students know nothing about a topic, they are understandably reluctant to answer questions about it. If we boost their content knowledge, we build their confidence to tackle the material. Short nonfiction offers both useful background information and practice in reading nonfiction. But simply providing information is not usually enough to stimulate interest or engagement. When students *interact* with the information in some way, such as by predicting or making judgments about it, this interaction enables them to "own" the ideas.

Because many other books have covered this ground (see the Recommended Reading chapter at the end of this book), I will provide brief summaries of various effective strategies.

Give the Trailer

Doug Lemov notes that one way moviemakers inspire us to go see their movies is by providing trailers that excite our interest, and teachers can do the same for books.[22] To hook students on *Macbeth*,[23] for example, he notes how people today still use the expression "having blood on your hands" as a sign of guilt—even though Shakespeare created it four hundred years ago. You can tell your students that they are going to read this scene that "people have found unforgettable for centuries." When they encounter the scene, they'll pay extra attention to it. My friend Steve Chiger, who teaches high school English at North Star Academy, has extended this idea a bit further: he gives students provocative lines from each act, then has them invent a story that goes around them. He notes: "This approach sneakily highlights some key lines. The giant poster I made that says, 'Blood will have blood,' doesn't hurt, either."[24] To which I would respond, *Hey, whatever works.*

Brainstorm and Categorize or Cluster

Brainstorming helps students plug into what they already know about a topic or issue.[25] Along with jogging their own memories, as they listen to their peers' ideas, they will notice that they actually know more than they thought they did. One caveat: how you frame the topic or question makes a difference. Open-ended questions can be more effective because they cast a wider net than text-specific questions. For example, asking students what they think "The Scarlet Letter" means might not generate much of a response. By contrast, "Jot down everything that comes to mind when you hear the word *red*" works well to introduce Hawthorne's classic. If you ask them to determine logical categories that their brainstormed words or phrases fit into, students will gain practice in analyzing and explaining—that is, using their inference skills. In addition, the categories suggest topics or issues that students can keep track of while reading.

Fast-Write and Everybody Writes

Traveling down the same road as brainstorming are two related options, Fast-Write and Everybody Writes.

Laura Robb describes Fast-Write as "a writing strategy in which students write about a topic for a few minutes to reclaim what they know."[26] She calls it "a safe cognitive warm-up" and frames it primarily as a way to identify what students recall about a topic, noting that "it can be a springboard for discussions and provide you with data that inform instructional planning." I like the concept of "reclaiming" ideas so that students can remind themselves that they actually do know something about the topic and can wrestle with it more confidently.

Along similar lines, Lemov describes Everybody Writes as a way to "set your students up for rigorous engagement by giving them the opportunity to reflect first in writing before discussing."[27] This description sounds more analytical than the recall-oriented strategy that Robb describes, though perhaps they are merely two sides of the same coin. On a DVD clip, Lemov shows the example of Art Worrell of North Star Academy asking students, "What are some of the characteristics or qualities that an individual must have to change history?"[28] Although some students might be able to blurt out responses to such a question, giving them all time to reflect and refine their thinking can lead to more robust discussions and more thoughtful writing.

Both techniques can certainly be used before, during, and after reading. I mention them here so that you can start using them right away.

KWL (What I Know–Want to Know–Learned)

Although many folks believe that KWL is an effective before-reading strategy, I agree with Lemov that it can be problematic because students tend to generate inaccurate "facts" in the What I Know column and don't know enough to ask useful questions for the Want to Know column.[29] We will revisit this as a during-reading strategy.

Anticipation Guides

Anticipation Guides are not as elaborate or cumbersome as they might sound.[30] They're simply lists of controversial statements (relevant to the text or unit in question) that students must agree or disagree with—such as, "Lying is never a good idea." (*But what if the dress is really ugly?*) The primary purpose is to raise students' awareness of issues in the text or unit and engage them in the suspense of wondering how these issues will be addressed.

The key challenge for teachers when constructing Anticipation Guides is to avoid claims that are obviously right or wrong (such as, "Hitler was a bad person"). Beers looks for "the big ideas or themes that are presented" in the text or unit and creates several statements of belief that are debatable. For example: "Good deeds are always rewarded" and "Children should be obedient to their parents even if it means having to do something they don't want to do."[31]

Depending on how much time you want to devote to discussing students' thinking on these statements, you can use the Anticipation Guide before, during, and/or after reading.

Predict, Preview, Analyze, and Connect

Many teachers ask students to make predictions about the text before reading, which can be a simple, useful strategy as long as the predictions truly are *predictions* and not guesses. Predictions are based on *evidence*; guesses are based on nothing. Meteorologists study cloud formations and wind direction; they don't just stand in front of cameras and make up stuff. Guesses are pointless because they do not require thought. Also, incorrect guesses can make matters worse by introducing inaccurate information, which some students will remember as "facts." Asking students to speculate about how *Mary Poppins*[32] will end when they haven't read any of it is a waste of time. By contrast, if they look at the cover, which features a woman with a suitcase in her hand apparently using an umbrella to fly, they should be able to infer that the main character might have some tricks up her sleeve, particularly when it comes to transportation.

The strategy of predicting works not only with fiction and drama but also with nonfiction because social studies, science, and math involve problems with consequences and solutions that can be predicted. Robb refers to a related approach (used with nonfiction and textbook passages) as Preview/Analyze/Connect.[33] Students examine text features such as headings, captions, and boldface words in order to analyze them and make connections. Students work in pairs or small groups to share their observations and connections. This process is more elaborate than predicting because it invites students to become more personally invested in the text by making Text-to-Self Connections (which we will discuss in detail in the During-Reading section later in this chapter).

Think-Pair-Share

Last, but definitely not least, is my favorite all-purpose strategy for engaging students in *any* material, whether before, during, or after reading. Think-Pair-Share is simple, effective, and efficient. You ask a question and give students time to think and/or jot down a note, then invite them to share with a partner, then cold-call to launch a whole-class discussion. This technique enables you to hold *everyone* accountable for thinking and learning, not just the students who raise their hands. From the students' point of view, even if you didn't initially think of anything, you've had a chance to hear someone else's idea, so you should have something to say. Lemov provides a thorough explanation of why and how cold-calling works as an engagement strategy (not a discipline strategy),[34] so I won't delve into the details here. Suffice it to say that the room is more lively when everyone is engaged. Extroverts (who often become frustrated when their class participation is reined in) find a valuable channel for their energy and inclination to verbalize thoughts when they can share ideas with a partner. And everyone's voice is validated, even if only by one other person. Everyone in the room gets a chance to speak and be heard.

Here's one additional tip: to increase the rigor of Think-Pair-Share, ask students to report out what their *partners* said. The first time you do this, be sure to warn them in advance. Requiring them to report out on a routine basis trains them to listen to one another instead of just waiting for the other person to stop talking so that they can talk. It also sends the message that everyone must contribute to the learning in this room.

DOGGIE BAG

1. Which of the before-reading strategies described here do you already use with your students?

2. Which before-reading strategy would help your students the most? Why?

DURING-READING STRATEGIES

The first step to solving any problem is to acknowledge that there is one. Far too many students do not understand that it is their job as readers to monitor their own comprehension. This is the first problem: they don't even notice when they're not comprehending.

I suppose it shows what a literacy geek I am that one of my favorite passages of all time is Cris Tovani's description of the day she realized that students were depending on her to tell them when they didn't understand what they were reading. She then asked them how they knew they were confused and what they did when they were confused. She reports, "Their responses made it clear that they didn't recognize confusion until they had to do something with the information, like answer questions or write a summary. Not until they tried to remember what they had read did they realize they weren't comprehending."[35] Like Tovani's students, many readers fail to notice they are stuck until after they have finished clawing their way through a passage. Then it's too late. Confused and frustrated, some ask for help; some give up. Many believe that they are not good readers and never will be. They believe that good readers never struggle.

So, for teachers, **Step 1 is to make sure students understand that good readers monitor their comprehension and acknowledge their confusion, that this is a skill that *everyone* can and should develop.** Also, it's a necessary life skill: most jobs require you to pay attention to what you're doing; if you don't monitor your thinking, the quality of your work will suffer. If you're a daydreaming bus driver or crane operator, you could put yourself or others in danger.

Step 2 is teaching students how to recognize when they're stuck. How do you know when you're stuck? For me, it's usually when I suddenly notice that I've "read" the past two pages and have no idea what I read. Possibly something in the text made me think of something else, so I started thinking about that while my eyes kept moving on autopilot, "reading" but not really reading. I have to go back and reread, this time fully attending to the text, asking questions, and drawing inferences as I go.

Tovani teaches her students six signals that will indicate when they're stuck.[36] The wandering mind is one. Others include not being able to hear your internal reading voice, which asks questions and draws inferences (as opposed to simply reciting the words); not being able to visualize what's going on in the passage; not being able to remember what you've read; not being able to answer questions that you ask as you read; and not being able to recognize a character who reappears (which, if you're reading a Russian novel, is almost inevitable).

Once you realize you're stuck, Step 3 requires you to do something about it. Tovani recommends the following "fix-up strategies."[37]

- Make a connection between the text and:
  - Your life
  - Your knowledge of the world
  - Another text
- Make a prediction.
- Stop and think about what you have already read.
- Ask yourself a question and try to answer it.
- Reflect in writing on what you have read.
- Visualize.
- Use print conventions.
- Retell what you've read.
- Reread.
- Notice patterns in text structure.
- Adjust your reading rate: slow down or speed up.

Read-Alouds and Think-Alouds

In addition to teaching these "fix-up" strategies, we need to *model* what good readers do via read-alouds and think-alouds. In *The Read-Aloud Handbook*, Jim Trelease makes the case for reading aloud to children from birth, noting that if you would talk to a child who couldn't understand a word you were saying, why wouldn't you read to that child for the same reason?[38] He points to data that show a positive correlation between reading aloud and phonemic awareness, language growth, beginning reading skills, and vocabulary acquisition.[39] Unfortunately, many children—especially those from low-income homes—are not read to at home. Teachers can make up lost ground and inculcate future generations in the value of reading aloud by beginning early with this approach. Teachers and school leaders should also consider presenting parent workshops on the importance of reading aloud. Trelease's chapter on the Do's and Don'ts of Read-Aloud would make a great handout.[40]

Taking reading aloud from the home into the classroom, Harvey and Goudvis describe interactive read-alouds, in which students listen to the teacher reading and discussing the text.[41] The teacher invites students to activate background knowledge (either alone or in pairs), then models her thinking and notes the strategies she's using. Students take notes, then the teacher shifts the responsibility for thinking to students, who work in pairs then report back to the whole class.

Harvey and Goudvis note that while the listening approach in interactive read-alouds improves comprehension, it does not improve fluency since the students are not doing the actual reading.[42] By contrast, when students read independently, they improve both comprehension and fluency.

Along the same lines as interactive read-alouds, think-alouds demonstrate out loud what effective readers do in their heads so that students will be able to recognize effective comprehension strategies and deploy them when reading. You begin with before-reading strategies, and students have their own copies of the text, ideally to take notes on, as they read along. Beers notes that it is critical to model think-alouds with different genres: "I can't presume that just because I've modeled how I think through a poem, students know how to think through a persuasive essay."[43] Repeated modeling is essential.

On a practical level, Daniels and Zemelman recommend warning students that you are going to stop and think as you read, then shifting your voice when you stop to think so that they notice the difference.[44] Other techniques can also work: Beers notes that she likes to shift how she's holding the book, and some teachers turn their bodies in a different direction or say, "Thinking now," or "My turn."[45] Students should track the strategies you're implementing in some way. Beers suggests: "When you've finished your think-aloud, let students go back and decide if you were predicting, commenting, noting your confusions, deciding how to fix up what confused you, questioning, clarifying, or visualizing as you read."[46] *If they can recognize the strategies, they are moving in the direction of using them.* Then give students opportunities to practice thinking aloud with a partner, to apply the strategies directly. Last but definitely not least, invite students to reflect on how thinking aloud has affected their reading habits.

Read with Purpose and Focus Groups

In addition to modeling effective strategies, it's vital to ensure that students always read with purpose. One of the worst classes I ever sat in went like this: "OK, everybody, let's turn to page 57. David, please read." David read haltingly while his classmates alternately doodled, stared out the window, or put their heads down. This went on seemingly forever. I wanted to put pins in my eyes.

We can debate about the pros and cons of having students read out loud in class, but there is no question that whenever one person is reading, everyone else should be, too, and each student should be reading with *questions* in mind. If David's teacher had said, "Let's see if we can figure out how Willy Loman feels about Biff in this next section. As we read, please jot down any clues you notice," then maybe I wouldn't have felt like blinding myself. One key to successful whole-class analysis of texts is that the teacher must be extremely well prepared. You can't just walk in and turn to page 57. By scripting questions and anticipating conflicts, revelations, and other highlights to notice, you bring urgency and enthusiasm to the discussion and ensure that every student is engaged. It helps to think of students as detectives: *What should they be looking for? What should they be trying to figure out?* It's our job as teachers to train them to read with a sense of purpose.

In addition to scripting questions for whole-class discussions, Gallagher recommends using Focus Groups to tackle longer texts.[47] As the title suggests, he puts students in small groups and gives each group a particular focus. Which lens they apply depends on the genre they're reading. With a novel, different groups might track different literary elements, such as "how setting (time and place) is used to develop emotional effect." Groups might also track different characters or historical figures. After the class has chewed through a significant chunk of the book, each group presents its findings while the others take notes.

One caveat about using Focus Groups: like anything else, the devil is in the proverbial details. Make sure students are crystal clear about their responsibilities. Groups can easily be derailed when they are uncertain about the elements they are supposed to track. For example, if students don't know what you mean by "major and minor conflicts," they might spend more time arguing about those definitions than looking for examples.

Twenty Questions

In addition to reading with purpose, students must read with determination and persistence. When the going gets tough, they can't walk away. One way to capitalize on students' confusion with challenging texts is to require them to generate twenty questions about the first chapter. As Gallagher notes, this approach conveys the idea that good readers acknowledge their early confusion and work through it.[48] By saving their first twenty questions and revisiting them, students will find the answers they sought and see the value of pushing through the difficult parts in a quest for clarity.

Making Connections to Self, World, and Text

We have already discussed the value of activating background knowledge throughout the comprehension process. Keene and Zimmerman, among others, recommend making text-to-self, text-to-world, and text-to-text connections for this purpose.[49] When students are able to recall relevant personal experiences, facts, or ideas about other texts, it can help them construct meaning from the text at hand.

However, not all connections are created equal. "The narrator has a grandmother, and I have a grandmother, too!" is not necessarily a meaningful connection. As you may have noticed, elementary school students have a tendency to launch themselves from their seats to volunteer such tidbits. Harvey and Goudvis caution: "These connections in common may in fact be important to the reader but not important to understanding the text." To address this concern, they offer a three-column form with the headings My Connection, Important to Me, and Important to Understanding the Text.[50] Forcing students to consider how much their connection helps them understand the text gives them practice in critical thinking and can lead to deeper insights. For example: "The narrator lives with her grandmother, and I do, too. She misses her parents, but she loves her grandmother, and this is important to me because I know how she feels. It helps me understand why she is so sad when her grandmother becomes sick, because I care deeply about my grandmother, too, and I'd be sad if she got sick."

Annotation

Over the years, students have taught me many vital lessons. Najla was no exception. Here is the story. Not long after we began to implement data-driven instruction at North Star Academy (a high-performing school in Newark, New Jersey, where I worked with Paul Bambrick-Santoyo, who later wrote *Driven by Data*), my colleagues and I in the Humanities Department sat down to analyze the results of the second Critical Reading Assessment. The results weren't pretty. The assessment was designed to target the critical reading portion of the PSAT and SAT, and the questions were not easy. A few students did well, though, so we knew it wasn't impossible. Figuring that the ubiquitous robust vocabulary had tripped up students, we decided to teach them fifty to sixty SAT-type words that would appear on the next test, then we'd be able to see if the problem was the vocabulary or something else. We also decided to teach them how to annotate: to underline the thesis or topic sentences, star supporting details, circle unfamiliar vocabulary words, note questions in the margin, and summarize the passage.

A quick sidebar: I was very proud of the posters I made and distributed with directions on how to annotate until a few days later, when a history colleague came to me and said that when annotating for homework, her students had circled lots of words, but then hadn't bothered to guess the meanings or look them up! She solved that problem by instituting open-homework quizzes; students instantly realized they would do much better if they noted synonyms and definitions.

After the third assessment, we looked at the results and were again disappointed. Overall, scores had not improved very much. But when we looked more closely at the data, we noticed that several students had improved *dramatically*. In particular, a tenth-grader named Najla had jumped from 35 percent on the previous assessment to 67 percent on this one. To put this in perspective, given the difficulty of the test, 67 percent was considered an A. Only two other students had outscored Najla. What made this even more striking was that Najla was not an A student. At the time, she was not even a B student. But she worked incredibly hard and would do anything you asked her to. A classic example of what Carol Dweck would call someone with a "growth mindset,"[51] she was determined to succeed.

So, burning with curiosity, we dug through the pile of tests and pulled out Najla's.

It didn't take us long to figure out what Najla had done: she'd annotated the *heck* out of the test! She had written all over it, underlining main ideas, starring supporting details, noting questions that occurred to her. . . .

We were convinced. In true North Star fashion, we vowed to teach annotation more aggressively in every subject, assigned annotation for homework every night, and *required* students to annotate on the next assessment (if they didn't, they'd have to stay after school for three hours and retake the test).

Annotation works. And although it might take a little extra time, it's time well spent, and it's a study skill our students will need if they are going to be successful in college. Following are a few annotation rubrics from the TLC Web site. Check out the TLC "Nonfiction Reading Strategies" page for additional resources.

Reading Standards	Points	Comments
Main idea or argument You underlined the main idea or argument in each paragraph.		
Details and evidence You have successfully identified supporting details. You have starred (*) two to three key supporting details per paragraph.		
New vocabulary You have circled all words that are new or unfamiliar or for which you do not know the definition.		
Questions and comments You have successfully added question marks to areas of confusion. You have successfully added comments that strengthen your understanding of the text.		
Total:		

What is the main idea or argument of this piece? Write one to two sentences.

_____

_____

_____

Write at least two questions you still have after reading the article.

_____

_____

_____

Annotation Rubric: Fiction and Narratives[53]

1. What question are we trying to answer? (such as "What type of character is
   _____?")

   _____

   _____

2. Underline or star details that answer this question.

Reading Standards	Points	Comments
Details and Evidence You have successfully identified details that answer Question 1. You have starred (*) at least _____ key supporting details per page.		
New Vocabulary You have circled all words that are new or unfamiliar or for which you do not know the definition.		
Questions and Comments You have successfully added question marks to areas of confusion. You have successfully added comments that strengthen your understanding of the text.		
Total:		

3. Write a thesis statement or topic sentence in response to Question 1 above
   (such as "Willie Loman is confused and angry.")

   _____

   _____

   _____

   _____

The illustration here shows an annotation system for math,[54] designed by fifth-grade math teacher Thomas Garza.

ANNOTATION SYMBOLS for FIFTH-GRADE MATH

Annotation System Key

C: circle numbers.
U: underline math vocabulary.
B: box the question.

Example 1: Ms. Boone asked her students to write (five) numbers to form a <u>pattern</u>. Darren wrote the <u>pattern</u> below.

(35, 70, 105, 140, 175)

On the lines below, [explain Darren's <u>pattern</u>.]

Example 2: Emily collected (two) different types of seashells. Of the <u>total</u> number of seashells in her collection, (20 percent) are cone shells. The rest are tulip shells.

[Write a <u>decimal</u>] that is <u>equivalent</u> to the <u>percent</u> of cone shells in Emily's collection.

No matter what annotation system you decide to use, keep in mind that marginal notes are more effective than highlighting. Students have a tendency to indulge in highlighting too much—or as I like to call it, coloring. And as incoming Harvard students are warned, although highlighting might seem like an active reading strategy, "it can lull you into a dangerous passivity."[55] When you go back to review the material, you'll be thankful when you've taken marginal notes and don't have to reread everything that is yellow.

In cases where students are not permitted to write in the books, sticky notes can work. Graphic organizers are also handy. More on these options in the section on Textbook Reading later in this chapter.

How to Find Topic Sentences

As we just mentioned, when annotating nonfiction, you must be able to find the topic sentence, which expresses the main argument in a paragraph. For this reason, in nonfiction, most body paragraphs should have one. Of course, not all writing is good writing. Textbooks are notorious for stringing along facts and occasionally indenting (see the section on Textbook Reading later in this chapter).

And even in good writing, when nonfiction writers take creative compositional risks, not all paragraphs have topic sentences. Still, students need to know (1) what topic sentences are, (2) why they are so important, and (3) how to find them. (PS: Students also need to know how to *write* effective topic sentences, which we will address in Chapter Three, in the section What Students Struggle With the Most When They Write.)

Review the section on Inferring Main Idea or Argument (AKA Summarizing) in Chapter One for details on how to teach students how to find topic sentences.

Visualizing

Often when people fail to understand something, they'll say, "I just can't see it." Visualizing is something that most of us do automatically. We read a story and begin to picture the characters and setting; as we start to "see" the action, the words become a movie in our head. As Robb points out, though, visualizing is not only for English or language arts classes: "In content area subjects, visualizing can help students recall a sequence of information, solve and/or graph a math problem, test their comprehension of new vocabulary, or draw and label diagrams, graphs, and experiments in science, and maps in social studies."[56] Harvey and Goudvis note that sketches can be particularly handy when making comparisons. For example, when you're trying to estimate the size of a Tyrannosaurus tooth, "as big as a banana" means more to a kid than "six and a half inches."[57] Indeed, drawing a picture—turning words into images—is a form of paraphrasing. In short, every student needs to practice visualizing. Enough said. Picture me dusting off my hands.

KWL (What I Know–Want to Know–Learned)

As noted earlier in the section on Before-Reading Strategies, using KWL when students don't know very much can be stressful because they know very little, and what they do "know" often isn't right. But once they have some background knowledge, KWL can offer a useful way to dig into the material and track student learning. The logistics are fairly simple: record students' brainstorming for each category on a separate chart, keep these charts posted in a highly visible location, and refer back to them as needed. Daniels and Zemelman note that sometimes students need help in generating questions about what they want to know—possibly because they haven't had enough practice in asking questions or don't want to seem ignorant.[58] You can solve both of these problems by encouraging a spirit of inquiry in your room, teaching students about the value of having a "growth mindset"[59] (that is, that working harder makes you smarter), and giving them lots of practice in questioning.

DOGGIE BAG

1. What key steps must readers take to monitor comprehension and deal with confusing passages?

2. Which of the during-reading strategies described here do you already use with your students?

3. Which during-reading strategy would help your students the most? Why?

TEXTBOOK READING: HOW TO MAKE LIFE LESS PAINFUL FOR EVERYONE INVOLVED

Because textbooks have made so many teachers and students miserable for so long, textbook reading deserves its own personal chapter. What's wrong with textbooks? It's not just that they're heavy and expensive and students aren't allowed to write in them or that, instead of modeling good writing with paragraphs that include topic sentences, they simply string facts together and occasionally indent, although these are all good reasons not to like them. Textbooks suffer from two main problems. First, they try to do too much at once. No matter what the subject, they tend to be overstuffed with information and difficult to decipher. Second, students need to be trained in how to read them, and far too many teachers skip this step.

"How do they get to ___ grade and not know how to read a textbook?" If only I could earn Frequent Flyer miles every time I heard this question. Just because students have been able to carry them around for years, that doesn't mean anyone ever taught them how to *use* them.

It's our job to take students as they are and move them forward. That means teaching them strategies in how to pull the most meaning out of what some might consider dense paperweights.

Step 1 is for teachers to take responsibility for the use of the textbook. This means deciding what role it will play in your class. Is it a resource, or is it the whole curriculum?

I recommend Door Number 1.

In my first year of teaching (at an affluent suburban public high school), for each assigned grade I was handed a textbook, a vocabulary workbook, and a "curriculum" that outlined authors and genres I was supposed to "cover." The curriculum provided no guidance about what I was supposed to *do*, so I spent a lot of time making up stuff. I relied heavily on the textbook and initially put a lot of faith in its premade tests and quizzes—too much faith, it turned out. About two weeks into September, my grandfather passed away and I had to take a day off for the funeral. We'd been reading "The Monkey's Paw," by W. W. Jacobs, and one class was ready to wrap it up, so I decided to give them the textbook-made quiz. I left copies for the sub and expected everything to go smoothly.

The next day I returned to a classroom thick with righteous indignation. I took a closer look at the quiz and realized that the students had a point: several questions *did* have more than one right answer. I apologized for the torment, told them I wouldn't count the quiz, and we talked through it. It wasn't lost on me that had I actually *taken* the quiz or designed it myself, we wouldn't have had this problem. Lesson learned.

So—the textbook cannot be your sole curriculum, and you need to check the resources that go with it. Some teachers' manuals can be remarkably helpful—if you take the time to scrutinize them. More on this topic in a moment.

What strategies should you emphasize in order to maximize what students can learn from a textbook? Keep in mind that students will probably need some background knowledge even before cracking the book. The before-reading strategies we've already discussed definitely apply here.

Next, you have to teach students *how to use the textbook*. By framing textbooks as a genre, you can point out the typical features of this genre and note how handy they are. For example, most textbooks include a table of contents, an index, and a glossary. Many make liberal use of boldfacing and italics to emphasize key terms and provide photos, graphs, charts, or illustrations to demonstrate key concepts. Many also include sections "for review" and questions or problems to solve. No doubt, these points will sound very obvious to anyone reading this book, but we should not expect that students already know how to derive meaning from such features. We must model how the four key critical reading skills—paraphrasing, inference, use of context clues, and summarizing—apply to each feature. We should not assume anything. In one science class where I taught a model lesson, not long after we'd spent ten minutes analyzing two pictures in the textbook and drawing numerous inferences from them, several students admitted that they had "barely ever even looked at the photos before." They were amazed that examining the photos helped them understand the ideas in the chapter!

Bottom line: Textbooks can be handy, but only if students know how to use them.

HOW TO USE THE TEACHERS' MANUAL

Teachers' manuals can provide considerable direction in how to walk students through passages, but sometimes they can be as dense as a rainforest. Use this checklist as a guide:

❑ **1. Preread the passage.** What background knowledge will students need, and how will you activate or provide it? Also, think about essential questions that could be journal topics for the week. Consider themes and topics to which students can make connections.

❑ **2. Identify vocabulary words that students need to know in order to understand the story.** These should be Tier 2 words[60] for the most part. Prepare this list for students. To introduce the words, give them a chart with the word, the word in a sentence, and a place to speculate about the meaning, as demonstrated here:

Word [with space to write more information about the word]	*Sentence using word:* circle the context clues.	*Speculation:* What do you think this word means, judging by context clues?
ailment	She had an ailment that prevented her from talking.	

Review the section titled Vocabulary in Context (and Vocabulary Instruction) in Chapter One for more tips on vocabulary instruction.

❑ 3. Note places where the teacher's manual recommends stopping and use those prompts, which refer to skills that should be emphasized. When reading *anything* with students, you should provide questions so that they are reading *for a purpose.*

❑ 4. Design or prepare any graphic organizers that seem suitable for analyzing the text. For example, T-charts, Venn diagrams, Webs, timelines, Somebody-Wanted-But-So. . . . Be prepared to explain to the students *why* they are using *this particular organizer* for this text. Not everything can be explained with a Venn diagram! Make sure that one of your objectives is that "students will be able to explain which graphic organizer is appropriate for the given task in order to use graphic organizers effectively when analyzing texts."

❑ 5. Decide how you will check for understanding informally. For example:

- "Up to this point in the text, what do we know about _____? How do we know this? What's the evidence?" (As a reminder, the Common Core Standards place heavy emphasis on the use of evidence.)

- "How would you describe _____ so far? Why? What evidence can you provide?"

- "What is the problem or conflict? How do we know this? What's the evidence?"

- "Can you connect what's happening in this passage to something you've experienced?"

- "What do you think is going to happen next, and why?"

❑ 6. Look at the section on preparing for formal assessment, and decide what you want to do. Examples may include:

- Essays

- Open-ended responses and/or multiple-choice questions

- Vocabulary assessments (see the TLC "Building Robust Vocabulary" page)

- Various projects (maybe a group project)

- Check out the after-reading strategies later in this chapter.

THE TRUTH ABOUT TEXTBOOK "READING" TESTS

Again, I'm not saying no one should use textbooks. But here is a little story that may give you pause. One day, I was sitting with a group of fifth-grade teachers who had just given their students a reading-level assessment, and one teacher said, "I don't understand these results. According to this assessment, most of my students are reading at the third-grade level, but they get As and Bs on their reading tests."

"Tell me about those reading tests," I said.

"They're multiple-choice and some open-ended, based on the stories we read in class."

"So you read them aloud in class and discuss them fully?"

"Yes, and we let them listen to the tape, too."

As gently as I could, I pointed out that those textbook "reading" tests are not *reading* comprehension tests; they are *listening* comprehension tests. Students who pay attention in class *should* do well on them, no matter what reading level they are on. If you teach the passages strategically, students might build comprehension skills and become stronger readers. But if you've discussed every aspect of the text in class, the test doesn't really test their independent reading skills. It tests their ability to listen and remember. And while listening skills are necessary (see the section on Why Oral Fluency Matters in Chapter Four), they are not sufficient. Students need to be able to read and analyze passages completely on their own.

So how can you assess reading comprehension? On a regular basis, require students to read short (700 to 1,000 words) passages, preferably nonfiction, and give them critical reading questions to answer. See Connecting Key Critical Reading Skills to Test Prep Instruction in Chapter Six for a recipe on how to design critical reading questions.

AFTER-READING STRATEGIES

As we design curriculum—from units to lesson plans—we always want to keep the end in mind: What do we want students to know and be able to do as a result of this work? Therefore, *before* you start reading something with your students, you should decide why they're reading it and what they're going to do with it. In other words, how will they demonstrate understanding of the text?

DOGGIE BAG

1. How do you currently use textbooks in your class?

2. What are your students' biggest challenges when it comes to textbook reading?

3. What might you change about the way you use textbooks in order to improve your instruction?

Again, the "text" could be a story, novel, play, poem, article, textbook chapter, or math word problem. Or it could be a chart, a graph, a political cartoon, an artifact, a song, a dead frog, a bowling ball, or a set of chemicals.

In any case, we need to plan ahead and include time for comprehension practice along the way. It is not solely the job of English language arts teachers to teach students how to comprehend. *If we all target the four key critical reading skills, our students' ability to comprehend in every content area will increase dramatically.*

I've devoted large chunks of this book to an array of literacy-based assessments. If you want to give students practice in speaking and listening, check out the sections Socratic Seminars Made Easy and Book Talk Projects in Chapter Four. Writing in response to texts can be done in various ways. See Chapters Seven (The Document-Based Question Approach), Eight (Research Paper Guide), and Nine (Teaching with Novels).

In addition, next are a few other suggestions for after-reading strategies.

RAFT: Retelling in Various Perspectives and Genres

Daniels and Zemelman recommend the RAFT (Role, Audience, Format, Topic) approach because it gives students a menu of options for what and how to write in response to a reading.[61] You offer students various *Roles* (so that they can write from the point of view of a famous person they have just studied), *Audiences* (relevant parties, whether groups such as newspaper readers or other recently studied individuals), *Formats* (such as editorials, poems, or letters), and *Topics* (relevant to the reading). Depending on whether the students are ready for this, you can develop the categories all by yourself or with some brainstorming from students, or they can design the charts on their own. An example of this approach follows.

Role	Audience	Format	Topic
John Adams	George Washington	Personal letter	Explaining why Washington should be president
Abigail Adams	John Adams	Personal letter	Explaining what is going on in their neighborhood while he is away in Paris
George Washington	John Adams	Personal letter	Reflecting on what he learned as president
John Adams	Newspaper readers	Op-ed piece	Critiquing Jefferson's first term in office as president

Because this is an exercise not only in writing but also in demonstrating understanding of content, it's important for students to share their results in some way, whether in small groups or with the whole class.

Mystery Envelopes

A close cousin of the Focus Groups described in the preceding During-Reading Strategies section is another group activity that Gallagher suggests. Students focus on something particular related to the text: a single intriguing question for the group to answer.[62] For example: "What is the single most important word in this chapter, and why?" Gallagher notes that each group in the class may be given the same question, or they might all have different questions. In either case, the mysterious envelopes should generate both intrigue and robust discussions. Then groups share their responses while the rest of the class takes notes.

Group "Exams": Make 'em or Take 'em

Giving students an opportunity to design "the test" (or parts of it) in groups is one way to review material. But be careful: this activity can become chaotic and unproductive if the directions about the nature and kinds of questions you're looking for are too fuzzy or ambiguous. It's vital to establish clear, specific parameters. Here are a few examples:

- Design twenty questions about the characters in Zora Neale Hurston's *Their Eyes Were Watching God*,[63] including at least ten multiple-choice and five open-ended questions.
- Create six essay questions about the American Revolution.
- Create five word problems that involve distance, rate, and time.

I also require students to provide the correct answers or "bullet points of information that should be included" in the case of open-ended or essay questions.

When it comes to "taking 'em," Gallagher recommends giving groups a premade multiple-choice test with one answer sheet; this approach forces students to come to consensus on answers.[64]

However you frame the process—that is, whether groups make the test or take it—they *must* have a chance to discuss what they've learned and clear up any misunderstandings.

DOGGIE BAG

1. Which of the after-reading strategies described here do you already use with your students?
2. Which after-reading strategy would help your students the most? Why?

READING WORKSHOP: SOMETHING TO CONSIDER

While many English language arts teachers have woven writing workshop into their classes, reading workshop is still far from the norm. I have a theory about this, and it stems from something Donald Graves reportedly once said to Nancie Atwell, the author of *In the Middle*. Graves is widely regarded as one of the forefathers of writing workshop, and one day he came to visit Atwell's class in rural Maine. After spending the day with Atwell and her students, he told her, smiling, "You know what makes you such a good writing teacher? You're so damned organized." He explained that her ability to run "a tight ship" enabled her to teach reading and writing so successfully. Reflecting on his feedback, Atwell notes: "A workshop is a different kind of ship. From the beginning of my attempts to teach using a workshop approach, I've had to organize and reorganize my room and myself to support writing, reading, learning, and teaching." She says that organization is not strictly about neatness, but "discovering what writers and readers need and providing plenty of it in a predictable setting."[65] Workshop teachers are very much facilitators who know how to put their hands on what their students need. Workshop teaching is a high-maintenance proposition.

On this point, my theory is that teachers, like anyone else, go through phases of growth. Early on, you're trying to get your bearings, trying to figure out what resources you have and how to use them. Typically you don't know what you don't know. Depending on where you teach, you may or may not have the resources you need, which adds to the challenge. Then you have to figure out how to improve on what you've developed. You need training in new techniques, and you need to find effective ways of organizing what you've learned and what you're trying to accomplish. Because the workshop approach requires a sophisticated set of organizational strategies to be effective, it requires extensive training and support. Rookie teachers are usually more focused on classroom management and don't receive workshop training; in fact, some teachers *never* do. And while you can read numerous books on how to run a reading or writing workshop, it certainly helps to have some training and see a workshop in action before diving into it yourself.

If I had to pick one to start with in elementary or middle school, I'd go with writing workshop, because teachers often have enough reading materials to work with but aren't quite sure what to do about writing instruction, so the workshop approach provides a clear sense of direction. Then, once you've mastered that, you can apply the same techniques with reading because they both follow the same basic format: mini-lesson, individual work with conferencing, and sharing session. Reading workshops typically focus on comprehension strategies and how to conduct accountable talk[66] (which we'll discuss further in Chapter Four, on speaking and listening).

To avoid redundancy in this book, I've described only writing workshop in detail (see the section called Writing Workshop 101 in Chapter Three), but you can learn more about reading workshop on the TLC "Reading Workshop" page.

I also recommend the following books:

Atwell, N. (1998). *In the middle: New understandings about writing, reading, and learning* (2nd ed.). Portsmouth, NH: Heinemann.

Calkins, L., and Tolan, K. (2010). *A guide to the reading workshop: Grades 3–5.* Portsmouth, NH: Heinemann.

Lattimer, H. (2003). *Thinking through genre: Units of study in reading and writing workshops 4–12.* Portland, ME: Stenhouse.

Miller, D. (2009). *The book whisperer: Awakening the inner reader in every child.* San Francisco: Jossey-Bass.

DOGGIE BAG

1. Why should you consider using a reading workshop approach?

2. What are the challenges when using a reading workshop approach?

3. How might you adopt some aspect of reading workshop in your class?

TLC DOWNLOAD ZONE FOR READING

K–12 ELA Common Core Standards Tracking Sheet

What's Important Organizer

What's Important Organizer Model

Generic Annotation Rubrics for Fiction or Narratives and Nonfiction

Writing

READ WELL TO WRITE WELL

If you skipped the reading section thinking, "Let me just see what she has to say about writing instruction," think again. The first thing I want to make clear is that we must *read* well to write well. I learned this the hard way. In one of my lowest moments as a teacher, not long after I collected the research papers that my students had spent a full month writing, I discovered that they resembled a town in the aftermath of a tornado. A few "buildings" remained standing: the papers had thesis statements and properly cited quotes and Works Cited pages. But other than that, they made no sense: you couldn't picture a town there. I realized then that the problem wasn't what I had taught; it was what I'd *assumed* they already knew: how to read documents and determine what was important and which pieces of evidence would best support their arguments. I hadn't taught that. So we went back to the proverbial drawing board. We worked on reading strategies so that we could improve our writing.

Writing requires reading for two main reasons. First, you can't write about *nothing*. You need a topic and specific information. Say you want to write about bravery. You'll need prior knowledge, which can come from experiences that are direct (such as trying to run for the first time several months after I ripped my Achilles tendon) or vicarious (such as reading about how it feels to climb Mount Everest). Either way, you'll use words you learned from having read them somewhere else. Which brings me to my second point: reading provides models of good writing. As I like to tell my students, good writers steal ideas all the time: they learn how to write by imitating other good writers. Our job as teachers is to show students models worth emulating. More on this approach in the Teaching with Mentor Texts section in a moment, later in this chapter.

WHY WE WRITE (AND READ)

All writing is not created equal. The next few pages explore the key purposes of writing, what we try to accomplish with different genres, and how metaphors enrich our writing (and our understanding when we read).

The Four Purposes of Writing

Why do we write? Other than "because my teacher said so," writing has four main purposes. Probably because I am a fan of desserts and love the notion of "pie" as a verb, I like the acronym IPIE (for Inform, Persuade, Inspire, Entertain).

Students need to be aware of these general purposes both as they're reading and as they're writing so that they can comprehend texts and create them. The author's purpose is in the same bucket as the main idea or argument,

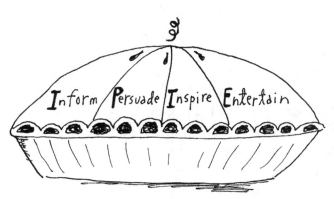

after all. Whether you're trying to figure out what that purpose, idea, or argument is or trying to convey one yourself, you need to know what your options are.

It's important to note that persuasion (discussed in more detail in Chapter Five) is inherent in all four purposes, because even when we are attempting to inform, inspire, or entertain, we are also attempting to convince the reader of something: to understand information, to believe in a cause, or to think we're funny. No matter what we write, we're trying to prove some kind of point. The following is one way to frame this concept for students.

What are we trying to accomplish when we write?		
	What We Do	**The Basic Structure**
Nonfiction	Make an *argument*.	Argument + Evidence That Proves It + Explanation
Fiction or Narrative	Convey a *message*, *lesson*, or *insight*.	Theme + Story That Illustrates It

On the flip side (or maybe on another poster), the reader's job is to figure out what the writer's argument or message is. Students who can see that reading and writing are two sides of the same coin are better able to analyze texts and create texts that accomplish these various purposes.

Why We Use Metaphors

Another way to illuminate the connection between reading and writing is to show students how and why we use metaphors.

If I am honest, I never really thought about *why* we use metaphors until the day one of my colleagues came across the hall and asked for help. Her tenth-graders were reading *Hamlet*,[1] and she'd asked them to identify uses of rhetorical devices and explain why Shakespeare used them.

"Great!" I said. "So what's the problem?"

She brought me into her classroom and asked a student to repeat his answer.

The boy nodded and said, "Hamlet says, 'Denmark is a prison.' That's a metaphor."

"OK," my colleague said, "so why did Shakespeare use that metaphor?"

"Because it's a comparison of two unlike things, saying they're similar," he replied.

"Aha," I said, exchanging a glance with my colleague, who gave me a look as if to say, *See what I mean?*

"That's the definition of *metaphor*," she said, "but that's not *why* he used it. Why do you think he used it?"

"Yes," I chimed in, "why didn't he just say, 'Denmark sucks'?"

The class giggled, but no one could figure it out. I thought for a moment, then wrote *prison* on the front board. "OK, everybody. Take ninety seconds and write down everything that comes to mind when you see this word."

PRISON

They bent their heads and wrote furiously. Unfortunately, many of them knew a lot.

When we wrote their ideas on the board (*punishment, locked up, torture, oppression, lack of freedom*, and so on), they realized that the word *prison* evokes many more feelings and ideas than "Denmark sucks" would have. People with different background knowledge about prison react to the word differently and thus form different interpretations of Hamlet's statement. With just one word, the metaphor adds layers of meaning.

I pointed out that this example demonstrates why everyone's reading of a text is different: our varied experiences and knowledge lead us to understand the text in different ways. Good writers use this fact to their advantage and choose words with care.

This is what our students learned that day: *metaphors are tools that multiply meaning and give readers more to think about and more to feel*. They give our writing greater impact. That's why we use them.

PUNCHY INSIGHTS, OR HOW TO AVOID WRITING LIKE A ROBOT

So far, we've talked about the purposes of writing and how metaphors convey meaning to readers. Now let's consider the bottom line. If you think about why we *read* books, magazines, newspapers—really, anything other than a grocery list—it's because we want to learn something. We want to understand something we didn't grasp before, or we want to know more about something, to know it more deeply. Whether reading fiction or nonfiction, we're looking for an argument or a message—something that makes us say, "Aha." In short, we're looking for insights.

Unfortunately, many well-intentioned elementary and middle school teachers who want their students to write well ignore this point. Instead, they provide students with formulas that result in—you guessed it—formulaic writing. Students follow their directions perfectly and end up writing things that are perfectly dull. For reasons that I have never understood, many teachers have relied on this dictum: "First, tell 'em what you're gonna say, then tell 'em, then tell' em what you told 'em." You can spot the results a mile away. They include phrases such as "I'm going to," and "My first reason is, my second reason is . . ." then a conclusion that repeats the thesis, often verbatim.

My gut reaction when I see this kind of writing is *Argh*.

I want to tell these teachers: *You are not helping! Your students might be able to write basic, boring paragraphs and essays, but now I have to undo all of their robotic habits and teach them how to write something that people would actually want to read. Why don't you just do that in the first place?!*

There, I've said it.

Now, how can I help? Let's return to the primary goal of any decent piece of writing: to express an insight. How can you elicit insights from, say, a third-grader?

Believe it or not, it's not that difficult. The first step is clarifying that this is what good writers do: they convey arguments, messages, and lessons. So readers should look for these arguments, messages, and lessons. For instance, you could say to your students: "Let's think about the story we read yesterday. What lesson did we learn from 'The Emperor's New Clothes'?[2] What was the author trying to tell us?"

To the same extent that students can understand what they read, they should be able to express that understanding orally and in writing. If you ask them inference questions while reading, they will draw inferences that ultimately add up to insights about the text. However, if you limit yourself to the bottom level of Bloom's Taxonomy with literal comprehension questions such as "What is the setting?" and "Who are the main characters?" then you should not blame students for failing to draw inferences. As noted in the section on Inferring Main Idea or Argument in Chapter One, the main idea or argument is an *accumulation* of inferences. So you have to start with one inference at a time, brick by brick, until you have a recognizable structure, something that makes you say, "Aha!" or at a minimum, "I know what that thing is."

One way to steer students toward insights is to ask them questions that—wait for it—elicit insights. My "Punchy Insights Poster" on the TLC "Writing 101" page does just that. I encourage students to respond to one of the following questions in their conclusion.

Punchy Insights[3]

- Message or lesson learned?
- Broader implications for all of us?
- Connections to my values, hopes, or dreams?
- How will this piece change how people think?
- What does the author want us to remember?

Depending on what grade you teach, you might want to modify this poster. Some teachers have reworded it as a series of sentence starters—such as "The author of this story wants us to remember _____." Others have kept the questions but altered the vocabulary. It might also help to post sample insights about texts that students have read. Like this: "In *How the Grinch Stole Christmas*,[4] Dr. Seuss wants us to remember that Christmas is about more than just gifts and presents."

Active reading leads to more effective writing. The drive to find insights when reading increases the likelihood that students will convey such insights in their own writing. And it's crucial that we point out to students that *this is the goal of good writing.* Revealing insights is what you want to do when you write.

As we prepare instruction to illustrate this point, we must be thoughtful about which texts we point students toward, to ensure that they'll care about the texts. Ralph Fletcher offers this wise reminder in *What a Writer Needs*: "You don't learn to write by going through a series of preset writing exercises. You learn to write by grappling with a real subject that truly matters to you."[5] When we help students connect with readings or subjects that truly matter to them, they'll find the insights they need to write about.

DOGGIE BAG

1. Why must we read well in order to write well?

2. Why do we write? What are we trying to accomplish?

3. Why do people use metaphors?

4. How can we teach students to avoid writing like robots?

5. What new lessons will you teach your students about writing?

A SIMPLE RECIPE FOR WRITING INSTRUCTION

Some of my favorite foods are not difficult to prepare: grilled salmon, scrambled eggs on toast, chocolate milkshakes, that sort of thing. Good writing instruction doesn't have to be complicated, either. No matter what genre you're teaching (whether it's a paragraph, a timed essay, or a full-blown research paper), I recommend the following basic steps:

1. **Explain to students which genre they are about to work on and why.** Ideally you'll have a good hook, not just, "We're writing this essay because it's Tuesday."

2. **Provide an excellent model and preview the scoring rubric, then use the rubric to critique the model, annotating it as you go.** Keep a running list of the compositional risks or techniques that make the model successful—in other words, what works. For example, "use of strong vocabulary" and "effective transitions leading to smooth flow" will probably appear on most lists.

3. **Invite students to critique models of varying quality so they can see the characteristics of effective and ineffective writing.** Evaluating different samples will help them become comfortable with the rubric and your expectations for the assignment. It will also train them to be more self-critical when revising their own writing.

4. **Explain why prewriting is so important, and hold students accountable for using prewriting strategies.** Particularly on timed essays, students tend to skip prewriting because they believe it's better to write for the entire allotted time. However, what often happens to students who don't plan or outline their ideas is that they write frantically for ten minutes and then, like a sprinter who suddenly runs into a wall, they abruptly run out of things to say. (PS: I like to demonstrate this with the nearest wall because it gets students' attention.) Then they spend the next twenty minutes in agony. Our job is to teach them how to avoid hitting that wall. Along with teaching them the needed strategies, we must hold them accountable for using them. Grades signal what we value, and students will take prewriting more seriously if you assign a grade to it.

5. **Teach prewriting strategies.** For most writing assignments, the biggest challenge is generating an appropriate topic and argument or message. The next section (What Students Struggle With the Most When They Write) explains how to tackle this challenge. Students also need to know the goals of the task, which graphic organizers to use and *why*, and, if it's a timed task, how much time to spend on prewriting. Model every step of the prewriting process *repeatedly* and walk students through plenty of guided practice before giving them independent practice. *Note:* Some teachers make the mistake of skimping on the "I do" and "We do" phases of the lesson, thinking that they will save some time. They won't. Students who haven't seen enough modeling tend to struggle with their independent work. Then you have to go back and reteach. So it's better to take the time up front and set students up for success.

6. **Give timely feedback on the actual writing.** If you're teaching the writing process and have the opportunity to support students along the way, you

should read their introductions and make sure they're on the right track before continuing. It takes less than a minute to determine whether a student has drafted a viable thesis, but there is no telling how long it takes to undo his frustration if he has spent hours writing a whole essay, only to be told that the thesis makes no sense. With very brief conferences, you can redirect students toward more productive lines of thinking. If students are working on a timed essay, it's best to grade the whole thing as soon as it is done and give students a chance to revise it using your feedback. The lessons they learn from improving that essay will prepare them to do a better job on the next one. And if they can't figure out how to fix *this* one, how can we expect them to do better on the next one?

7. **Last but not least, require students to reflect on their strengths and weaknesses as a writer.** One way to support this self-reflection is to provide students with feedback and hold them accountable for following up on it. In the forthcoming section on Rubrics and How to Spend Less Time Grading, you'll find an Essay Writing Rubric that includes a separate grade for Self-Improvement Goals. Sometimes it helps to remind students that you won't be going to college with them, so they'll need to learn how to improve their writing on their own. The sooner they learn *this* lesson, the better.

DOGGIE BAG

1. What does effective writing instruction look like?
2. What might you do to improve your writing instruction?

WHAT STUDENTS STRUGGLE WITH THE MOST WHEN THEY WRITE

While it might sound simple to say, "Teach students how to develop insights so that they can write about them," the devil is, as always, in the details. Having a valid point doesn't mean it's easy to write clearly and cogently. Students often struggle mightily even when they know what they're supposed to do. The good news is that we can anticipate their challenges and set them up for success.

Argument versus Evidence Revisited

As noted in the section on Inferring Main Idea or Argument (AKA Summarizing) in Chapter One, students often conflate argument and evidence when reading, a problem that inhibits their comprehension. This problem obviously also affects their ability to *write* effective arguments supported by relevant evidence. Therefore, while we need to teach them the difference when reading, we also need to reemphasize this distinction when students sit down to write. Following the aforementioned directions in Chapter One is a start. Then you'll need to train students in how to find and write topic sentences—that is, the paragraphs' main arguments—and how to find and provide relevant evidence.

Topic Sentences Revisited

The quest to write effective topic sentences reminds me of an old TV commercial—I think it was for tacos—in which people argued, "I like making them!" versus "I like eating them!" In the case of topic sentences, you must know how to *find* them before you can *write* them. So this section reviews the process from soup to nuts. Or, if you prefer, soup to tacos.

Strategies

1. **Teach students to identify and underline the thesis or topic sentence.** Given passages, use the I Do, We Do, You Do approach[6] to practice this skill. To learn more about this, read the section on Inferring Main Idea or Argument (AKA Summarizing) in Chapter One.

2. **Give students sample effective topic sentences for which they must generate relevant evidence.** Bullet points are OK to start; later they can add the rest of the paragraph. Model this, then have groups try it and report back to the whole class. Then let students do it independently. *Hint:* For struggling students, one way to scaffold this skill is to provide a topic sentence with evidence options and have students rate the effectiveness of each piece of evidence. As always, be sure to model this skill; inexperienced readers have limited exposure to effective writing, which is another reason why they don't know what "good" supporting evidence looks like.

3. **Give students a list of effective and ineffective topic sentences and ask them to infer what makes them effective or ineffective.** Ineffective topic sentences suffer from these common problems:
   - Fact, not argument
   - Too broad or general ("Everyone knows" ...)

- Too specific (not much you can say about it)
- Irrelevant to the thesis (if one is given)

Sample Resources

See Evaluating Topic Sentences: *I Know Why the Caged Bird Sings* by Maya Angelou on the TLC "Effective Topic Sentences" page. This handout reveals the most common problems, so you might want to use it first. If your students haven't read that book yet, create your own handout based on something they have read.

See also Evaluating Topic Sentences: *The Street* by Ann Petry on the TLC "Effective Topic Sentences" page for more practice.

---

4. **Give students paragraphs that include effective and ineffective evidence and ask them to infer what makes the evidence effective or ineffective.** Ineffective evidence suffers from these common problems:

- Irrelevant to topic sentence
- Self-contradictory
- Inaccurate or imprecise (such as hyperbole)
- Not convincing (relevant but not compelling as support, causing readers to ask "So what?")

5. **Give students effective topic sentences about texts they are reading or have read, and require them to write the rest of the paragraph with effective evidence for support.** This approach came to me when I was trying to accomplish three things: (1) I wanted students to demonstrate understanding of the text, but I also wanted to avoid short-answer questions because they tend to generate low-level and easy-to-copy responses; (2) I wanted to strengthen students' writing skills in general; and (3) I wanted students to practice quoting, explaining, and citing sources. I knew it was important for students to see a model of what I expected, so I provided one (based on a chapter from Judith Ortiz Cofer's collection of interconnected stories, *An Island Like You*[7]) at the top of every handout. An example based on Esmeralda Santiago's captivating memoir, *When I Was Puerto Rican*,[8] follows. *Note:* See the TLC "HS English Lessons & Units" page and "MS English Lessons Units" page for more examples of paragraph response handouts.

Directions: For *each topic sentence* given, write a paragraph proving it, and cite at least two direct quotes from the chapter. Each paragraph must be seven to ten sentences long (including the topic sentence). Be sure to cite the page numbers properly. See the model. Attach loose-leaf if needed. Be sure to read the whole chapter before writing a paragraph.

Example

In the beginning of the story, Kenny's mother makes it clear that she does not respect his friend Harry. When Harry shows up to invite Kenny to his party, Kenny's mother is "furious" that Harry is in her house (82). She follows Kenny into his room to tell him why he should not be hanging around with such *"basura"* (82). She says that Harry acts like "the devil, tempting innocent barrio girls and boys with free drugs and easy living until they [are] hooked" (82). She goes on and on about how Harry's behavior is wrong. She says that people who follow Harry "pay the price" (82). She is obviously worried about how Kenny's friends will influence him.

1. Negi does not always obey her mother, and on several occasions her disobedience leads to negative consequences.

Hints

1. Use content that you want students to learn or review, so the reading serves two purposes.

2. You don't have to be Ernest Hemingway! It's not always necessary to create sample paragraphs from scratch. When possible, use preexisting texts and simply doctor them to suit your needs. But be careful: textbooks can offer lousy models. They often lack topic sentences; instead they tend to string facts together and occasionally indent. Magazine articles are often more useful.

3. After students have written their own paragraphs, use their (anonymous) examples as teaching tools.

THESIS BRAINSTORMING AND ORGANIZING

It amazes me that anyone can write an entire essay without a thesis. But I've seen it done. I think this is why so many students hate to write. They pour hours and hours into pages and pages, only to be told that what they've written is unacceptable. *After all that effort: unacceptable?* Sadly, yes. An essay without a thesis might have half a dozen great ideas in it, but without an organizing principle, it doesn't hold together.

Our job is to spare students (and frankly ourselves) this agony by coaching them on how to write an effective thesis. *The solution is to give students practice and not let them go any further until they've generated a viable thesis.* Once they've got it, then they can move on to the rest of the piece. Otherwise, you'll need to spend more time conferencing with them. (*Note:* In the upcoming Writing Workshop 101 section, we discuss how to conduct effective conferences). Eventually, with enough practice, they'll get the hang of it.

Although there are numerous ways to arrive at a thesis, it helps to have a systematic approach to start with. Following is one for an essay based on a text.

Brainstorming for Your Thesis[9]

1. **What *topics or issues* does this text deal with?** List as many as you can think of. (Example: *How the Grinch Stole Christmas!* by Dr. Seuss[10] is about *selfishness, generosity, love, and personal growth.*)

2. **What *questions* does the author raise about these topics or issues?** Pick one to two topics to focus on. (Example: Why are people selfish? What are the consequences of selfishness? How can people overcome selfishness?)

3. **What *message(s)* does the author convey about your selected topic or issue?** Sometimes it helps to *find connections* among a few of your favorite topics and *explain them* in relation to the book. (Example: People can overcome selfishness with love from the people around them.)

Once students have pinned down a message or argument they want to focus on, they can craft a thesis. If writing about a work of literature, they should include the title, author, and specific aspect(s) of the book that convey this message.

Here are some sample theses based on novels:

- In *Their Eyes Were Watching God* by Zora Neale Hurston,[11] Janie, the main character, searches for equality and independence, and she learns some important lessons along the way.
- In *The Street*, Ann Petry[12] highlights the conflicts that Lutie has with Boots, Johnson, and Jim to show the difficulty that women, both married and single, have in constructing a life for themselves.
- In *The Street*, Ann Petry's characterization of Mr. and Mrs. Chandler underscores the subtle yet pervasive racism that plagues the whole African American community.

Once the thesis is in place, students can map out the rest of the essay. Here is a completed model of the "Unpacking Your Thesis Organizer"[13] found on the TLC "Writing 101" page.

This organizer can be adapted to suit other genres, as well. The key is to model *how to ask compelling questions* because questions drive the writing process from three angles:

1. Good questions enable writers to build strong arguments.
2. Good questions help writers to look for and find useful evidence.
3. Writers must ask good questions in order to analyze and support their arguments.

Initially, you'll have to provide the questions. Then you can remove the training wheels and let students generate their own. No matter what you're doing, you should begin by providing a model of what you're looking for. Which leads us to our next section, on Teaching with Mentor Texts . . .

Thesis or Argument Statement: In *Their Eyes Were Watching God* by Zora Neale Hurston, Janie, the main character, searches for equality and independence, and she learns some important lessons along the way.

What are the different parts of the argument that your essay must prove?

Janie searches for equality.	*Janie searches for independence.*	*Janie learns some important lessons.*
What questions must you answer to prove this part of your argument?	What questions must you answer to prove this part of your argument?	What questions must you answer to prove this part of your argument?
1. *Why does Janie have to search for equality?* 2. *How does Janie search for equality?* 3. *How successful is she at finding equality? Why? What does she learn?*	1. *Why does Janie have to search for independence?* 2. *How does Janie search for independence?* 3. *How successful is she at finding independence? Why? What does she learn?*	1. *What lessons does Janie learn?* 2. 3.
Write a topic sentence that answers at least one of the questions in the above box. *Janie searches for equality through her relationships with men.*	Write a topic sentence that answers at least one of the questions in the above box. *Because her relationship with Joe frustrates her so much, Janie relishes her freedom after he dies.*	Write a topic sentence that answers at least one of the questions in the above box. *Janie's struggles teach her some essential life lessons.*

DOGGIE BAG

1. What do students typically struggle with the most when they write?

2. What strategies do you need to teach your students to help them overcome these challenges?

TEACHING WITH MENTOR TEXTS

Whether you are teaching reading or writing, mentor texts can be tremendously helpful. This section answers the most common questions about them, namely: *What are mentor texts? Why do we need them? How can we use them effectively?*

What Are Mentor Texts, and Why Do We Need Them?

If you want to be a rock star, you can't simply read an instruction manual or listen to a lecture on how to do it. You need to watch rock stars in action. Just as we learn things from models, so do our students. In the field of literacy, the fancy term for a model is a "mentor text," which can be almost anything: a lab report, a research paper, a poem, a pie chart ... even something as brief as a punchy conclusion. Whether it's student-created, teacher-created, or work from a published author, it offers a shining example for students to emulate.

Mentor texts are more than simply models, however. They teach strategies. As Lynne R. Dorfman and Rose Cappelli explain in *Mentor Texts*, in order to help students become strategic learners, we must make strategies *visible* to the students. For example, you might say something like: "We have been working on how an author reveals his character to his readers, and I want to show you how I use this knowledge as I write."[14] The point of the mentor text is not merely to show something that works, but to show *how to do* that thing well.

Perhaps even more important, effective mentor texts (or role models) *motivate*: they make you want to imitate the model. You can see clearly what you have to practice, and you want to dive into that practice. In *The Talent Code*, Daniel Coyle tells the story of a thirteen-year-old girl named Clarissa, whose videotaped clarinet practice session he describes as "The Girl Who Did a Month's Worth of Practice in Six Minutes."[15] Clarissa was part of a study conducted by Australian music psychologists Gary McPherson and James Renwick. While reviewing the video, Coyle remarks at the quality of her "highly-targeted, error-focused process," and McPherson notes that she seems to have "a blueprint in her mind she's constantly comparing herself to."[16] Later, McPherson reveals what triggered Clarissa to undertake such intense practice: her teacher became frustrated while trying to teach her a new song and decided to play a jazz version of the song. Clarissa fell in love with this version, and "all of a sudden, she's on fire, desperate to learn."[17] The desire to imitate something great can spark a commitment to what Coyle calls "deep practice."[18]

Along these lines, one of my most memorable experiences with mentor texts as a student came in the graduate fiction workshop at Johns Hopkins, when our professor, Francine Prose, handed back our first stories and informed us that our sentences were "lying on the page like dead fish." The twelve of us gasped. Then she handed out a page full of compelling sentences to show what she wanted us to do. Though I wouldn't recommend using such a blunt introduction, I became much more vigilant about the quality and capacity of every single sentence I write as a result of Francine's use of mentor texts to challenge and inspire us.

So here's something to think about: *How compelling and inspirational are the examples that you share with your students?* If you want them to write great expository essays, have you shown them examples that make them passionately want to write? The more students *care* about the work, the more time and energy they will spend on practicing to improve their skills. Our job is to get them to think of themselves as *writers* so that when they read, they'll be on the lookout for good ideas, strategies, and techniques that will make them better writers.

How Can We Use Mentor Texts Effectively?

Mentor texts can be used for a wide range of purposes: to teach reading or writing strategies, to study genres, to model how to solve problems or apply the scientific method .... (*Note:* We will explore the role of mentor texts in genre study in the section Connecting Writing to Reading Through Genre Study in Chapter Six). In short, no matter what grade or subject you teach, you can find different ways to demonstrate specific strategies with your chosen mentor texts. The key is to decide what those strategies are, locate appropriate mentor texts, and design lessons or mini-lessons that will get your points across. One caveat: while traditional writing workshops include mini-lessons (described in the next section), Dorfman and Cappelli prefer "Your Turn" lessons, which utilize the gradual release of responsibility model, AKA the I Do, We Do, You Do approach advocated by Lemov[19] and others. Their rationale for the longer lessons is that "the mini-lesson format does not always provide enough time for students to understand the strategy and make it their own."[20] Whether you use mini-lessons or regular-length lessons, you'll need a stockpile of mentor texts to get your points across.

Now, if you are panicking at the thought of having to assemble a vast collection of mentor texts, here is some good news: Carl Anderson, author of *How's It Going? A Practical Guide on Conferring with Student Writers*, notes that you don't need to have fifteen different texts to demonstrate fifteen different strategies; in fact, it's quite possible to use the same text repeatedly for multiple purposes.[21] That doesn't mean you can slide by with just one, of course. Anderson suggests an array of potential sources: texts you've already read to students, excerpts from longer works, student writing, student- or colleague-recommended texts, and texts you've written yourself.[22]

No matter what strategy or skill you're trying to teach with a mentor text, be sure to carve out some time for student reflection. When students contemplate how a strategy has helped them, they experience a stronger sense of ownership of that strategy and are more likely to use it again. To this end, you should ask questions such as these: *How did the use of the strategy or skill work for you? How did it improve your piece? How will you revise the use of the strategy or add your own personal touch?*[23] The bottom line is that we want students to see themselves as learners who approach challenges with strategies, not empty-handed.

DOGGIE BAG

1. What are mentor texts, and why do we need them?

2. How compelling and inspirational are the examples that you share with your students?

3. How might you use mentor texts with your students more effectively?

WRITING WORKSHOP 101

In striving for a balanced literacy approach, more and more K–8 teachers have begun to incorporate writing workshop into their routines. Although I don't know many high school teachers who use writing workshop in their classes (probably because they tend to have less time than elementary teachers for literacy instruction), there are certainly aspects of writing workshop that high school teachers can and should adopt. I won't describe exhaustively how to run writing workshop because so many others (including those cited here) have already covered this ground. However, it is useful for our purposes to review the basic elements: (1) mini-lesson, (2) individual work with conferences, and (3) sharing sessions. Mentor texts play a key role in the mini-lessons (to model the strategy you're trying to teach) and in writing conferences (when you want to demonstrate specific skills). Let's look at each workshop element more closely . . . .

Mini-lesson

Mini-lessons are "compact vehicles" for teaching the content or skills that you want students to pull from mentor texts. *Lucy Calkins suggests an array of categories for mini-lessons:* launching the workshop, choosing a topic to write about, conference strategies, classroom procedures, rehearsal and revision strategies, qualities of good writing, and literature.[24] When applying a "genre study" approach to writing workshop, Heather Lattimer slices the "learning categories" pie in half: *text structure study* (because you need to know the conventions of the genre you're writing in) and *writing process study* (because writers in different genres "adapt the standard 'gather ideas, outline, draft, edit, revise, publish' process to fit their genre").[25] No matter which approach you take, you can plan ahead, but you should also expect to change your plans to meet students' needs—or, as my high school Latin teacher used to say with a wide grin, "Let 'flexibility' ever be our watchword!" Great teachers set high standards, observe students with care and vigilance, and adjust their plans as needed to ensure that students meet (or exceed) their standards.

Most mini-lessons follow this standard format:[26]

- *Connection*. Make a connection to work that students have been doing already. Name the teaching point.

- *Teaching*. Name the context that might lead a writer to use today's strategy. Use a mentor text to give an example of a writer using that strategy. Demonstrate how to use the strategy. Include bits of advice as you go.

- *Active engagement*. Prepare children to use the strategy you've just taught by helping them to imagine themselves in the situation that calls for that strategy. Then give them a brief chance to try the strategy, usually involving a Think-Pair-Share approach. Keep in mind that this is supposed to be a *mini*-lesson, so you want to be efficient. Calkins and Martinelli recommend soliciting or reporting on two examples, ideally ones you've overheard and vetted.[27]

- *Link*. Link the mini-lesson to students' independent writing, often by reminding them of what they've learned. After clarifying your expectations for their independent work, send them off to write.

(*continued*)

(*continued*)

Individual Work with Conferences

When students return to their seats to work independently, circulate and conduct conferences. You'll refer to mentor texts *and* function as a mentor yourself. It's important to remember that in this role as your students' mentor, you have tremendous power—which reminds me of my first day at the restaurant where I was hired to do salad prep. An older boy who'd been assigned to train me said, "Watch this." He grabbed a handful of mushrooms, tossed them onto a cutting board, and sliced them in five seconds without even looking at them. Then he handed me the knife. Before I could move a muscle, our boss appeared from nowhere and took the knife from my hand. "Just remember that this knife is very, very, *very* sharp," he said. "Take your time. You'll get it. But be careful." Unlike the modeling provided by my "trainer," his additional coaching probably saved me several trips to the emergency room.

Ralph Fletcher notes that a mentor must have high standards, build on strengths, value originality and diversity, encourage students to take risks, be passionate, and see the big picture. To that final point, Fletcher tells the story of how the midwife described his screaming, seemingly distressed newborn son as "a robust little boy" with "strong lungs." She helped him see his child differently, with pride. He reminds us that as mentors, "Our words will literally define the ways they perceive themselves as writers."[28] This is no small responsibility. And it offers a tremendous opportunity to inspire. I'll never forget the day that Ed Brown, my twelfth-grade English teacher, told us, "The great thing about writing is that every time you do it, you get better at it." What a liberating assertion! I thought: *I could get better at writing* every day? *My writing efforts will be rewarded? Wow!* That one simple sentence changed how I viewed the writing process and how much effort I poured into writing from that day forward.

What should you accomplish in a writing conference? Carl Anderson recommends a two-part structure: (1) Discuss the work that the student is doing as a writer, and (2) discuss how the student can become a better writer.[29] The teacher and student have different roles in these two parts,

(*continued*)

(*continued*)

with the student leading the discussion at first and the teacher directing the conversation in the second part.[30]

As for the instruction you should provide in conferences, Lucy Calkins wisely counsels, "Teach the writer, not the writing,"[31] meaning, *Teach strategies that they can use not just with this particular piece, but anytime they're in a situation like this*. So, you don't want to say, "You should put a comma here." Instead, ask, "Remember what we do when we begin a sentence with a dependent clause?" Which brings us to the content of conferences. Anderson notes: "Because writers do different kinds of work at different points in the writing process—rehearsal, drafting, revising, and editing—conferences focus on different issues at each point."[32] In short, what you focus on depends on what the student is working on. For more detailed information on how to conduct effective conferences, you should read Anderson's book.[33]

Sharing Session

After the independent work time, reconvene students to share their work—specifically, the work they did using the strategy of the day. Sharing should accomplish two key goals: (1) provide you with a sense of what the students understood and (2) reinforce the lesson you were trying to convey.

To be as efficient and purposeful as possible, you can't call on everyone (nor would you want to). So, how should you decide which child to call on? Either take a moment for students to share with a partner while you eavesdrop, or call on someone you noticed when conferencing. Select a student (or two, depending on the length of the piece they have to share) whose work exemplifies the lesson. Then, either ask questions to elicit an explanation of the strategy, or reflect on what you noticed in the writing.

Here's an example from Calkins and Martinelli of how to extract lessons (in this case, about revising endings) from one child's work: "Writers, did you notice that Jill reread her whole narrative, paying attention to what it was she really wants to say in her ending? Then she drafted three versions of an ending. Next she plans to take the best of all three—but she could have selected one. At the end of today, she'll have produced four lines of text—but that'll be a good day's work."[34] This highlighting of an individual

(*continued*)

(*continued*)

student's work not only reinforces the lesson, but also provides Precise Praise (Technique 44 in *Teach Like a Champion*)[35], which helps to build a culture of collaboration in the classroom. When students see that you value their efforts and that you will call on them to show what they know, they will grow to see themselves and their peers as *contributors to the collective learning*. This role gives them a sense of empowerment and ownership, and it also encourages them to listen to one another. More on this listening phenomenon in Chapter Four.

Whether you dive headlong into writing workshop or employ certain aspects of it in your writing instruction, remember to show models of what you're looking for. That's true for *anything* you want them to do. Which leads to our next point.

DOGGIE BAG

1. What are the basic elements of writing workshop?
2. Which aspects of writing workshop might you use with your students?

MOTIVATIONAL GRAMMAR

You may be wondering what grammar has to do with mentor texts. And I'm sure you're wondering how anyone could possibly put "motivational" in front of the word "grammar." Most people associate grammar with dread. Indeed, many of us grew up completing grammar exercises in textbooks or correcting sentences as part of the daily class routine. Now that we're teaching, we find that those approaches don't work with our students. They might earn 100 percent on a quiz about dependent clauses, but they don't use them properly in their own writing.

One thing we must do is show students *why* grammar—and punctuation, in particular—matters. Here's a quick way to illustrate this point: Compare "Let's eat, Grandma!" to "Let's eat Grandma!" In the first case, you're hungry. In the second, you're a cannibal. This example can be found all over the Web; I particularly like the one with the tagline "Punctuation saves lives!"[36] For more mature students, the "romantic" letters mentioned in the section on paraphrasing in Chapter One are also useful.[37]

Once we've established a sense of purpose, we need to employ an effective instructional approach. *Not* the "Daily Sentence Correction." Why doesn't that approach work?

First, the "instruction" (a term I use loosely here for reasons that will become obvious) often lacks purpose. It's not like, "Hey, we're working on comma rules today," it's more like, "Here's this wacky sentence; see if you can find three things wrong with it." Kind of a Where's Waldo activity for grammar mistakes. Here's a typical response: "It doesn't start with a capital letter! And *then* should be spelled *than*. And it ends with a question mark when it should end with an exclamation point!" Students don't learn strategies. At best, they are reminded of basic rules that they already knew.

What's even worse is that many teachers require students to copy down *incorrect* sentences, which is a *colossal* mistake. I repeat: *colossal*. Even though you might think they'll learn something from correcting the errors, the truth is that the original version will be partly burned into their brains. They might even walk away thinking the original form was correct. At best, the process of correcting will only neutralize the errors, not teach rules they didn't already know.

Fortunately, I've found a solution to this misguided approach: a terrific resource that actually gets students excited about grammar: *Mechanically Inclined: Building Grammar, Usage, and Style into Writer's Workshop* by Jeff Anderson.[38] Even if you do not run a full-blown writing workshop in your classroom, this book provides strategies that you can use. Anderson's main argument is that rather than correcting errors, students should practice *imitating what works*. He notes that daily correct-alls are rarely applied to students' own writing, which is why their lessons tend not to stick.[39] (Yes! Another reason to avoid them!) He explains and demonstrates how to take a "mentor text" approach to teaching sentence construction. He includes mini-lessons and lots of sample materials that are ready to use. No matter what grade you teach, you need to check out his book!

Following are a few other issues relevant to the realm of grammar.

Word Choice

As students attend to grammar and usage, they should consider how word choice conveys tone, mood, and perspective. One quick way to illustrate this point is to show students Dog Diary vs. Cat Diary[40] with its hilarious competing voices. The dog's diary begins, "8:00am: Dog food! My favorite thing! 9:30am: A car ride! My favorite thing!" while the cat's diary is titled "Day 983 of My Captivity" and begins, "My captors continue to taunt me with bizarre little dangling objects. They dine lavishly on fresh meat, while the other inmates and I are fed hash or some sort of dry nuggets." For more information on word choice, check out the TLC "Building Robust Vocabulary" page.

Transitions

As students attempt to write sentences that *flow* smoothly and coherently, they need to pay attention to their use of transitions. If you are frustrated with textbooks that define *transitions* merely as "time and order words," resulting in robotic student writing that relies heavily on "first, second, and third," here are two Web pages that provide a more nuanced explanation of what transitions are and how they work:

http://www.virtualsalt.com/transits.htm

http://www.studygs.net/wrtstr6.htm

DOGGIE BAG

1. What is the most effective approach to grammar instruction, and why?

2. What changes do you need to make to improve grammar instruction in your class?

RUBRICS AND HOW TO SPEND LESS TIME GRADING

Writing can take forever to grade. But it doesn't have to! This section looks at strategies that can save you time while still accomplishing your objectives. Probably the most helpful tool for grading more efficiently is rubrics. Once you've identified the key characteristics you want to evaluate, rubrics enable you to do it consistently. And they serve several other vital purposes, as well:

1. They communicate clear expectations to students and teach them academic language related to writing.

2. They provide a useful checklist for students to plan and evaluate their work.

3. They establish a common language for discussing writing across content areas so that teachers can have productive discussions about student writing and lessons. Indeed, even the process of trying to come to consensus on which rubrics to use can generate fruitful conversations about schoolwide expectations.

Of course, different genres require different rubrics. Generic holistic rubrics might seem efficient (which is why they're used on standardized tests), but ultimately they won't save time because at some point you'll have to provide the feedback and instruction that they don't.

The TLC "Writing Rubrics" page contains an array of rubrics for various genres. The following Essay Writing Rubric can easily be adapted for use across the curriculum.

Essay Writing Rubric[41]

Name:	Assignment:		
Writing Standards		Points	Comments
Introduction Engaging hook One to two supporting statements Thesis or main argument Thesis support statement			
Topic Sentences *Transition* from previous paragraph. Provide *argument* for the paragraph that answers *How?* and *Why?* in response to the thesis.			
Evidence Use *accurate* information and detailed support to prove thesis and topic sentences, including: *Context* surrounding the quote (who, what, where, when, and why)			
Quote or Paraphrase *Explanation* of quote and how it illustrates or proves the point			
Conclusion Draw logical, thoughtful conclusions and/or make reasonable predictions. Usually answers, "What is the author's ultimate message?"			
Proper MLA Citation Format *Parenthetical citations* in proper format			
Length Requirement _____paragraphs (or pages)			
Overall Persuasion, Coherence, and Depth of Analysis Build convincing paragraphs and an overall argument that flows clearly. Make thoughtful, logical, and substantial inferences throughout the paper. Anticipate potential counterarguments. Find meaningful connections.			
Grammar *Use standard English* (subject-verb agreement, present tense, and pronoun-antecedent agreement). *Punctuate properly.* *Structure sentences effectively.*			
Effective Use of Sophisticated Vocabulary **Subtotal**		/100	
Self-Improvement Goals		/20	

I love many things about this rubric:

- It enables you to put both the score and the comment right next to the specific element you're critiquing.

- It provides clear expectations (and you can assign different weights to different elements; they don't all have to weigh the same).

- It raises students' self-awareness by requiring them to generate self-improvement goals based on feedback from prior writing assignments. This final element came to me one day when I was lamenting to a colleague, "The problem is, I know what Shanique needs to do to improve her writing, but I'm not convinced Shanique knows." Let's face it: most students care mainly about the bottom line—their grade. They might also be interested in our comments, but unless they have to *do something about them*, they won't fully absorb the lessons we're trying to teach. This component requires them to identify what they need to work on and holds them accountable for showing improvement; they earn a separate grade for how well they do on the goals they've set. It forces students to take ownership for their own learning and growth as writers. In short, it's the writing equivalent of "monitoring comprehension."

The Journal Writing Rubric (which appears next and also on the TLC "Writing Rubrics" page) is useful across content areas when you want students to respond to a book, whether it's fiction or nonfiction, as they read it. You give students several open-ended questions per chapter, then score them according to the elements in the rubric.

Journal Writing Rubric[42]

Journal Writing Rubric Name: _____	Points	Three Journal Entries on _____ Comments
Argument or Evidence Respond directly and *thoroughly* to all questions. Build convincing arguments. Use *accurate* factual information and *sufficient* detailed support for arguments, including (for text responses). *Context* surrounding the quote (who, what, where, when, and why)		
Quote or Paraphrase *Explanation* of quote and how it illustrates or proves the point. Show thoughtful, logical, and substantial *inferences* in responses. Find meaningful connections.		
Grammar and Word Choice *Use language well* (sophisticated vocabulary, subject-verb agreement, and present tense). *Punctuate properly.* *Structure sentences effectively.*		
Proper MLA Citation Format *Parenthetical citations* in proper format (for text responses)		
Total		

Don't forget to check out the TLC "Writing Rubrics" page for other handy rubrics.

Grading writing clearly involves more than scoring. The type and extent of the feedback you provide is also critical to student learning. But you don't have to correct all of the errors you find on every single paper! In fact, you really shouldn't, unless you are practicing to become a copy editor. *Students learn from work they do. If you do all of the editing, you're doing all of the work.* To determine how much feedback to provide, you will need to answer the following questions:

- What are your objectives?
- What aspect(s) of the writing process are you emphasizing at the moment?
- How much scaffolding have you put in place to support your expectations?
- Will students have an opportunity to revise this draft?
- How will students make use of your comments in future writing?
- How will you hold students accountable for learning from their mistakes each time they write?

Once you've answered these questions, you should be able to determine your revision policy, which will in turn dictate the nature of your feedback. Keep in mind that your revision policy can either inspire or dishearten your students. As with many other things, I learned this one the hard way, and I was fortunate to learn it early in my career. After grading a disappointing set of essays from an honors-level class, I decided to offer my students a chance to revise the paper "up to a 70." It seemed like a fair solution: I didn't want them to fail, and if they wanted to get a better grade, they could. One parent, who happened to teach writing on the college level, came in to meet with me. Her son had earned a failing grade on the paper, but she wasn't there to complain. She agreed that he hadn't put enough effort into it. But she appreciated that I was giving him a chance to revise it. She had come in, she said, to talk with me about my revision policy—not as a mother, but as one professional to another. Then she pointed out gently that there was little incentive for students to do a great job on a revision when they knew they would only end up with a barely passing grade. She was right, and I knew it. I thanked her then, but I wish I could thank her again because this advice changed how I taught writing for the rest of my career.

Following are some revision policies to consider:

> • Revise for the highest grade possible.
>
> • Average the original and revised grades together.
>
> • Revise for a better grade up to 75 or 80.
>
> • Only people who failed can revise (and they have to sit with me after school to do so).

Your revision policy will dictate how extensively you comment on students' papers. If students cannot revise the paper, then there is little value in putting many marks or comments on the paper: a grade with a few sentences should be sufficient, especially if you are using something thorough like the Essay Writing Rubric featured earlier (and also found on the TLC "Writing Rubrics" page).

In some cases, revision can be optional. In some, it should not. Sometimes it makes sense to let students decide if they want to put more effort into improving their grades on a writing assignment. But when they fail to meet your minimum standard for a given piece, giving them an F doesn't accomplish the goal of teaching them to write well. That is why I invented the designation NGY—No Grade Yet—which requires students to sit with me for tutoring when their pieces fail to meet my standards for mastery. If they don't revise the piece, the NGY becomes a zero. (PS: Owing to my tendency to call their parents, very few students choose this option.) Although students dread receiving NGY, I think they also appreciate that it means they will actually learn how to write the piece in question and, after more hard work, can end up with a decent grade.

Following are some options for how much to comment:

- Write extensive comments on both the paper and the rubric, and fix errors.
- Write marginal comments and circle errors. Provide suggestions for improvement on the rubric.
- Put Xs in the margin next to lines where errors appear. Students should circle any Xs they don't understand, which they can discuss with you later, in conference. Provide suggestions for improvement on the rubric.
- Frame your comments as questions for the writer; ask students to answer those questions as an assignment. My friend Steve Chiger, who teaches high school English at North Star Academy, recommends this approach. Though he admits it takes more time, he believes that writing "What argument does this topic sentence make?" can be more useful than "This topic sentence states only a fact." When students have to discover the problem (with scaffolding) and take ownership for solving it, the results can be powerful.[43]
- Don't give feedback on the paper; provide suggestions for improvement on the rubric.

As you prepare any unit that involves writing, consider the following tips:

- *Plan backwards.* As Grant Wiggins and Jay McTighe like to say, start with the end in mind.[44]
- Provide models and rubrics to make your expectations clear.
- Explain the project's timeline and deadlines.
- Provide prewriting graphic organizers.
- *Collect the introduction and give immediate feedback on it before students go further. Without an effective thesis, the whole paper will suffer.*

DOGGIE BAG

1. Why do we use rubrics?

2. What do effective rubrics look like?

3. What factors should you consider when deciding how to grade and comment on an assignment?

4. How can you spend less time grading?

TLC DOWNLOAD ZONE FOR WRITING

Punchy Insights Poster

Essay Writing Rubric

Evaluating Topic Sentences: I Know Why the Caged Bird Sings by Maya Angelou

Evaluating Topic Sentences: The Street by Ann Petry

Argument versus Evidence: Catcher in the Rye by J. D. Salinger

Argument versus Evidence: President Harding

Argument versus Evidence: FDR

How to Find the Topic Sentence

Paragraph Responses: Sample, When I Was Puerto Rican by Esmeralda Santiago

Brainstorming for Your Thesis

Developing Your Thesis Organizer

Unpacking Your Thesis Organizer

Unpacking Your Thesis Organizer Model

Essay Outline Organizer

Journal Writing Rubric

Open-Ended Response Writing Rubric

Personal Narrative Rubric

Personal Narrative Project with Rubric

Poetry Explication Essay Rubric

Research Paper Rubric

Writer's Notebook Rubric

Speaking and Listening

chapter
FOUR

WHY ORAL FLUENCY MATTERS

Of all the ways you can improve learning in your school, the Number 1 way is to strengthen students' speaking and listening skills and habits.

Why? Let's start with listening. Probably at least 80 percent of what students do in any given class involves listening. And remember—by "listening," we mean *listening comprehension*. Whether listening to their teacher, their classmates, or some form of media, students must process and comprehend a lot of information aurally. *If they don't listen well, they won't learn well.* Therefore, we must train them to listen effectively. More on this in a moment.

Along these same lines, we must also teach them how to speak effectively. Obviously, speaking is an essential life skill in and of itself. But it is also crucial because of its impact on learning. *Active participants learn more.* Although it might sound really obvious, this truth took me a while to absorb and was finally brought home to me by one of my favorite students. An amiable high school student with Spanish-speaking parents, Jairo was fluent in English but rarely spoke up during class discussions. He almost never raised his hand. Before I began to use cold calling[1] to increase engagement, I made the common mistake of calling on only students with raised hands, so some students opted not to participate when they realized that someone else would do the work. Jairo took notes and appeared attentive, but he rarely volunteered ideas. Although confident in other ways, he lacked assurance in his academic abilities and avoided taking intellectual risks. In retrospect, I think he was stuck in a "fixed mindset" (a la Dweck[2]): he believed that he wasn't good at English and that was that. Then one night around 6:00 PM, while I was working with Jairo and a few other students on research papers, Jairo had a breakthrough: he was excited about his topic and had figured out how to explain it. He worked really hard and wrote a fabulous paper. A few days later, as I handed back the papers, I told everyone what a great job he'd done. From that day forward, Jairo opened up and began to engage in class discussions more assertively. One day when I praised him for his contributions to the class, he admitted, "I feel like I'm getting more out of the class when I say things." Indeed, he was. The quality of his work *overall* improved. If you ever feel like you don't want to push a shy child to speak up in class, think about Jairo. For far too long, I went easy on him, and he could have learned more if I'd expected more.

Effective speaking is also important because—along the same lines as writing—it demonstrates how much you comprehend. If you cannot articulate your thoughts coherently, it could be because you are not thinking clearly, you lack information, or you do not understand something. Or it could be because no one *expects* you to express your ideas fully, so you've developed a habit of expressing incomplete thoughts, which would also be bad.

Unfortunately, in many schools, incomplete thinking is widely accepted. Walk into a classroom in almost any school, and more often than not, you'll see a teacher calling on students who respond with incomplete sentences. It's a common occurrence for three reasons: (1) teachers want to keep things moving, so they often accept brief responses, (2) teachers' questioning techniques solidify into habits, and (3) most teachers don't understand the impact of this particular habit. The truth is, it undermines everything you're trying to teach because it derails the comprehension process. *When students don't explain their ideas with complete sentences, it may signal that they haven't reached the level of inference and explanation; they may not comprehend the topic, issue, situation, or point as fully as we would like.*

Students need to practice explaining ideas in order to become stronger *thinkers*. The act of explaining reinforces their inference skills and overall comprehension.

As noted in the section on inference in Chapter One, high standards for discourse in your classroom will boost not only fluency but also comprehension. Doug Lemov asserts that "the complete sentence is the battering ram that knocks down the door to college."[3] I would also add, "And it's great low-hanging fruit for teachers who want to help students improve their reading and writing." *The oral practice of expressing complete thoughts translates into more penetrating reading and more coherent writing, plus it teaches other students (who hear these complete explanations) more in the process.* It's a win-win-win.

To strengthen our students' speaking and listening skills, we must teach students *why* these skills are important, then *how* to do them. And they are clearly interconnected: if you listen well, you're better able to respond orally to what you've heard. In the next section, we'll look at how to train students to do both things well.

HOW TO TRAIN STUDENTS TO LISTEN AND SPEAK EFFECTIVELY

Because improving students' speaking and listening requires us to reshape behavior, change-related literature seems appropriate to consider. In their compelling, insightful book *Switch: How to Change Things When Change Is Hard*, Chip and Dan Heath describe an array of strategies to effect change, and two strike me as especially relevant here: "tweaking the environment" and "rallying the herd."

With the first strategy, you set up the environment so that it's easier for those involved to do what you want them to.[4] In our case, we need to make it easier for students to speak and listen effectively, and harder not to. For example, once students realize that you are not going to repeat and amplify what every student says, they will accept that it's easier for everyone else to hear if they don't mumble. And if they know that you are going to call on students to respond to one another, they will listen more avidly to what their peers say so that they won't look foolish when called upon. In a moment, we'll explore more ideas along these lines.

The second strategy suggests that people are more likely to do what you want them to if they feel like part of a group. The Heath brothers give the example that baristas and bartenders seed their tip jars because they are "trying to send signals about the 'norm' of the herd."[5] When you see that other people have left a tip, you follow suit. One way to create a "herd" in a classroom is to coach students on their collective identity, for example by affirming that "We're the kind of people who listen to one another and value what other people say." *If you want students to think of themselves as readers and writers, then call them* Readers *and* Writers *to convey this vision.* Many teachers take this approach in reading and writing workshops, but it works even if you don't teach with workshops. Then, any time you discuss "what good readers do" or "what good writers do," their ears will perk up, and they will latch onto the strategies that support their aspirations. To influence the habits of the "herd" more broadly, it also helps to use what Lemov calls "positive framing"—making interventions in a positive and constructive way—to guide student behavior.[6] Another technique for building a strong, supportive classroom culture is "props," in which students celebrate their peers' success by cheering them briefly and energetically (such as, "Two stomps for Imani!").[7] When offered up routinely, these props send the message that "We're all learning this together."

Now, here are a dozen things you can do to improve student engagement and strengthen their speaking and listening skills:

1. **Use Think-Pair-Share followed by cold-calling[8] as often as possible.** For example: "Take ___ seconds (or minutes) to jot down your thoughts about ____. [Wait the allotted time.] Now, take one minute to tell your partner what you thought. Then look at me when you're both ready to share with the class." Use popsicle sticks to cold-call, to ensure that you'll call on *everyone* eventually. Make it clear to students that you expect everyone to have something to say because they've all just written and talked about their ideas. When asking students to share, you can increase the rigor (and strengthen their listening skills) by asking them to report on what their *partners* said. Let's face it: when invited to "share with a partner," many students are simply waiting for the other person to stop talking so that they can say what they think. Their definition of listening, as my friend Katy Wischow once put it, involves "staring in silence." Having to report on their partners' ideas forces students to listen more carefully. It also gives them valuable practice in paraphrasing and summarizing. *Note:* the first few times you do this, be sure to warn students so that they are prepared.

2. **Encourage students to *restate or paraphrase*—not repeat—what their peers say.** If you ask them to "repeat" what others say, you miss an opportunity for them to practice paraphrasing. Repeating requires no thought. Also, repetition is boring—we heard it the first time. Make sure students know how to paraphrase and *why* it's important. When teaching students the value of paraphrasing—a vital conversational skill as well as a key critical reading skill—you might try the approach that Heather Lattimer describes in *Thinking Through Genre*.[9] Her colleague asks students to talk about how they responded to an excerpt from *Bad Boy*, by Walter Dean Myers, and each time after the first few students answer, she ignores what they said and instead tells her own reaction. The students become uneasy and reluctant to volunteer their thoughts. Then she calls on another student and paraphrases what he said before giving her own ideas. The students are surprised (and, quite frankly, relieved). Then she debriefs with the students on the different ways she conversed with students. They get the point: paraphrasing is a way to show that you are listening to the other person.

3. **Move from paraphrasing to inference as much as you can, and ask students for *evidence* to back up their ideas or arguments.** For example: "What can you infer from what Jairo just said? What evidence gave you that idea?" Teach

students how to paraphrase and infer early in the year so that they can log many hours of practicing these skills. Also, clarify the difference between argument and evidence. No matter what grade or subject you teach, even if the terms are not new to them, the review will establish a common language in the room. Posters can serve as handy reminders. The more students are invited to explain their ideas, the stronger their inference and comprehension skills will become.

4. **Treat students as sleuths.** Tell them that they are the Detectives, and you are the Clue-Provider. As I noted in the section on inference in Chapter One, Charlie Speck, my high school Latin teacher, was a master at this. He knew that if we had to figure things out, we would not only remember them but also be able to explain them. In his class, in order to catch all of the clues, we had to listen *very* carefully.

5. **Ask *why* as often as possible, to give students more opportunities to explain their ideas (which will boost their inference skills).** Even when they give the "correct" answer, ask them why because (1) they might have guessed and (2) their explanation will teach others in the room who might not have understood the material. *Note:* The first few times you ask why, students who aren't accustomed to being questioned might back away from their response or become defensive. I like to tell students, "I'm not asking why because I think you're wrong; I'm asking why because I genuinely want to know how you think and because your explanation will help your classmates understand this better."

6. **Require students to respond with *complete* sentences.** As noted earlier, this practice will enhance their fluency and comprehension. Explain why you have this expectation (which is for their benefit) to make it the *norm* in your class. Initially you might have to correct them a few times and model it or provide sentence starters, but students will quickly get the hang of it. I've taught sample lessons in classrooms where I made it the norm within five minutes. Set high standards for discourse in your room, and students will meet or exceed them.

7. **Don't repeat what students say.** Students are like cats who want more food in their bowl: they train us! If you allow students to train you to repeat what they say, then they won't develop proper speaking or listening skills. When you repeat what students say, it sends the message that they should not listen to one another. It also teaches them to mumble because they know you will amplify everything. Another downside is that repeating unnecessarily lengthens class discussions and undermines the ratio of student cognitive work.[10] Lemov

describes an array of methods for enhancing this ratio, including unbundling (asking numerous questions to dissect a topic or problem), feigning ignorance, and batch-processing (instead of responding to every single comment, responding after several have been made), among others.[11]

8. **Use think-alouds to model how you think, including the questions you ask and the way you figure things out.** Then you can invite students to pair up and practice their own think-alouds. Making thinking *visible* in this way makes it more accessible for everyone, especially those students who might otherwise believe that "some people just 'get it,' and some people don't." They will see that in fact reading and thinking *require work*. Good readers *wrestle* with the text.

9. **Invite students to *ask* questions as often as possible.** But this does *not* mean asking, "Does anyone have any questions?" for which the answer is almost invariably, "No." Instead, ask, "What questions could we ask in this situation?" or "What questions can we ask about ____?" Then write their questions on the board to show how much you value them. As a default, students need to know the utility of applying Five Ws and the H (who, what, when, where, why, and how) to pick apart texts.

10. **When reading aloud, require students to listen with a purpose or question in mind.** Reading aloud mindlessly is boring. It's an invitation to daydreaming at best and disruptive behavior at worst. But you can't blame the students; if you fail to engage them, they will find *something* to do. Spare yourself the agony by hooking them with a great question. For instance, invite them to make predictions based on evidence from the text so far. Then: "OK, let's see who's right!" and read the next bit.

11. **When lecturing or presenting new material, provide guided notes to keep students engaged.** In addition to keeping students actively involved, guided notes provide models of good note taking, another important skill. They also ensure that everyone walks away with the same basic information and a review sheet for later reference.

12. **Whenever a difficult-to-pronounce word appears, engage the *entire* class in choral pronunciation of the word.** It's highly probable that if one student mispronounces a word, others in the room would make the same mistake. In fact, if you correct this one person and move on, chances are good that the word will pop up again and someone else will stumble over it. So, it's better to spare this first reader the embarrassment and instead send a positive message to the whole

class, which is this: "This is an important word, and we *all* need to know how to pronounce it. So let's go."

Sample Choral Pronunciation Scenario

Student 1 (reading aloud): Some people advocated for "abol—?"

Teacher: Readers, this is an important word for us all to know and use. After me (*points to self*): abolition! (*Points to class.*)

Class: Abolition.

Teacher (*pointing to self):* Abolition!

Class: Abolition!

Teacher (*pointing to self*): Abolition!

Class: Abolition!

MORE THOUGHTS ON EFFECTIVE SPEAKING

Beyond requiring students to speak with complete sentences, we need to ensure that they develop a strong vocabulary and employ academic language to explain their ideas. Some educators refer to academic language as "accountable talk." No matter what you call it, it's crucial for several reasons.

Most obviously, having a common language supports smooth-running class discussions. Heather Lattimer notes that one of the goals of reading workshop is "accountable talk study." She explains: "Although not specifically a reading goal, talk is absolutely necessary to understand the text . . . Students must be taught how good readers discuss text, and they need to be taught the discussion formats and approaches appropriate to specific genres."[12] Of course, accountable talk is not limited to reading workshop. It needs to happen in every class and every subject because it prepares students for entry into higher-level discussions in college and the workplace.

However, this ability to wrestle with concepts using academic language is needed not merely for academic or professional conversations. How students speak to a large extent determines how they write. To strengthen their writing, we must strengthen their speech. As Jeff Zwiers notes in *Building Academic Language*, "Students who haven't read many texts full of academic language tend to default to their oral language patterns."[13] We need to model academic language orally and when reading and analyzing various genres so that students will have the tools they need to "enter the conversation," as they say, on the level of their academic peers—both orally and in writing.

How can we teach academic language? I recommend both Zwiers's book and his Website (http://www.jeffzwiers.com) which include many helpful suggestions, but I will highlight a few key strategies.

Provide direct instruction on the moves we make when conducting academic discussions. Teach students actual phrases that they can use, for example, to add to what a peer has said (such as, "I have two points that relate to what you said . . ."), to contradict or disagree politely ("That's a valid point, but I feel . . ."), to shift the focus, to analyze, to state an opinion, and to support a point with evidence.[14] Post these terms and phrases prominently, make reference to them, and encourage their use.[15]

Raise students' awareness of how they sound by modeling how to turn an informal conversation into a more formal, academic one. Provide a sample transcript with *before* and *after* statements so that students can see how to make their explanations more academic. For example: "They couldn't vote. It wasn't fair" becomes "African Americans didn't have the right to vote. This wasn't fair." As Zwiers points out, this technique can be used to teach or review concepts.[16]

Boost students' vocabulary by using words in context. As noted earlier, when you use words with enough context clues (such as "Who wants to help *disseminate* these papers?") or redundantly ("Halt, stop, cease, desist!"), students will infer their meanings and begin to use them. A few weeks after I'd given a workshop on vocabulary instruction at her school, a stunned kindergarten teacher told me that one of her students used the word *continuum*. When she asked him where he'd learned that word, he replied matter-of-factly, "You used it last week." Indeed, children absorb a lot more than we might expect. Rather than talking down to them or worrying that they won't understand what we're saying, we need to use strong vocabulary and instructive or directive context to build their word knowledge. In any given class, you might teach them five new words simply through the way you communicate.

Finally, keep in mind that academic language is not just about using big words. As Zwiers notes, "Students must also develop skills with the many 'smaller words' and grammatical conventions that make the big words stick together to make meaning."[17] Academic language is about syntax and grammar and how we explain ideas as much as it's about vocabulary.

CLASS DISCUSSION LOGISTICS

In addition to focusing on students' use of academic language, we need to pay attention to how we orchestrate class discussions to facilitate learning. Logistics are important. Following are two points to consider.

Two-Handed Discussions

We all love it when our students become so actively engaged in a discussion that we don't know who to call on next because we see so many hands in the air. One "problem" that sometimes arises is that while some students want to comment on what was just said, others may have new ideas to introduce. With so many hands waving, we don't know how to choose. Luckily, with the help of a student, I discovered a solution to this "problem."

One day while my seniors were discussing Toni Morrison's *Song of Solomon*,[18] the student leading the discussion was doing her best to call on everyone who wanted to speak, but several students were becoming frustrated. They wanted to respond to ideas that had been raised, but the topic kept changing. Finally, Aaron, who desperately wanted to respond to something that one of his peers had just said, raised *both* of his hands and leaned forward as far as he could.

Aaron's melodramatic gesture drew chuckles, and I suddenly realized that we could use his two-handed approach (but without the leaning-forward-and-moaning part) to make it easier to identify students who wanted to comment on what was just said versus students with one hand up who wanted to introduce a new idea. The students agreed, and from that day forward, it worked. Discussion leaders would scan the circle and say, "I see a few people with two hands up, so let's hear from them first before we move on."

Reporting Out

When students are engaged in group work, we typically require them to "report out" on their group's findings. Zwiers describes reporting out as "one of the most important yet underdeveloped stages of group work,"[19] and I couldn't agree more. Too often, we fail to model what we expect the "reporters" to do, fail to provide a rubric for this work, and fail to hold the audience accountable for listening (so instead they frantically continue preparing their report while ignoring whoever is presenting). As a result, students miss opportunities to practice effective presentation skills and learn from one another. We need to raise our standards both for the reporting and for the listening. Zwiers recommends some fairly obvious steps such as requiring all groups to stop preparing when it's time to report out and requiring listeners to take notes and ask questions; he also suggests setting up the presentations around the room so that students move around, become more engaged in note taking, and synthesize what they've learned.[20] Whatever techniques you adopt, raising and clarifying expectations for reporting out will help maximize student learning.

DOGGIE BAG

1. Why does oral fluency matter?

2. How can you train your students to listen and speak more effectively?

3. Which teaching techniques described in this section will help your students the most? Why?

SOCRATIC SEMINARS MADE EASY

One terrific method for training students in how to conduct intelligent conversations is Socratic Seminars. Students learn how to use effective habits of discussion, explain their ideas, and support them with evidence. Different educators have different ways of conducting Socratic Seminars. Here is my favorite recipe:

1. Direct four students to sit in the middle of the room, circled by the rest of the class. Everyone in the class has read the same text (whether story, article, editorial, or chapter) or undergone the same experience (such as a field trip or science lab). These four students are responsible for discussing a given set of questions on the text or experience for a given amount of time (I recommend ten minutes). *Note:* They are the only ones who speak; even you will not say a word once the discussion has begun. See the TLC "Socratic Seminars" page for the following documents: Socratic Seminar Questions on Persuasive Texts and Socratic Seminar Questions on Short Stories. These documents appear later in this chapter, as well. Also, consider adapting questions from the Book Talk Project for Class Novel; each group can discuss a different chapter.

2. At the same time, select four others in the outside circle to observe the four participants; the observers will complete a checklist and give feedback on their designated participant's performance. See the TLC "Socratic Seminars" page for Socratic Seminar Observation Checklist. This document also appears later.

3. Everyone else in the class takes guided notes on the discussion. (*Note:* Sample questions for guided notes are included in the question files, Socratic Seminar Questions on Persuasive Texts and Socratic Seminar Questions on Short Stories.)

4. Use a detailed rubric to score each of the discussants. See the TLC "Socratic Seminars" page for Socratic Seminar Rubric, which also appears later in this chapter.

5. After the discussion, invite the observers to share a few positive comments, then provide your own specific constructive feedback so that everyone in the room will learn more about how to do well.

6. Lather, rinse, repeat. Rotate the participants. Although you probably won't have time in one class period for every student to experience every different role, assure them that eventually they will all have numerous chances to discuss in the middle, be an observer, and take notes. *Note:* Plan ahead! Having a well-organized grade-recording system will make your life easier.

Tips for Introducing Socratic Seminars

- **Make a big deal about how important Socratic Seminars are for the skills they teach.** College students participate in seminars, and this practice—both the discussions and the note taking (a skill college students *must have*, but many struggle with)—will help them in the future.

- **Don't rush into the discussions without establishing your expectations for each role.** Explain the logistics fully and patiently. Take as much time as you need to clarify terms on the rubric, observation checklist, and guided notes organizer. Describe what a solid performance looks like—and, of course, sounds like—and be sure to emphasize that this is a group *discussion*, not just four people delivering monologues. How they respond to one another will affect their grade. Remind them to use strong vocabulary and academic language (or "accountable talk" or "habits of discussion," or whatever you call it), and point to any helpful posters for reference. Also, stress the importance of proper volume.

- **Customize the discussion questions and guided notes organizers as needed, but the rubric and observation checklist can stay the same.** It is generally best if different groups do not discuss exactly the same material (because the discussions can become repetitious and boring), but if they must, they should address it from different angles. For example, if you want five groups to discuss Elie Wiesel's *Night*,[21] give each group a different chapter or set of questions to tackle.

- **Make sure note takers have a clear picture of what good notes look like.** They did not emerge from the womb knowing how to take notes. Show them models. Teach them shortcuts and common abbreviations.

- **The observers' job is to provide positive feedback.** At least initially, it's best to limit observers' comments in the post-seminar debrief discussion to "what the person I observed did *well*." After each participant has received some positive strokes, you can offer "things to work on for next time." Later on, after you've trained students in effective *constructive* feedback, you can encourage that form of response.

- **To ease students' nerves the first time around, make the first time a "dry run" for credit and feedback, not a major grade.** While some students relish having an audience, others would rather flee the country. To accustom them to this potentially unsettling new ground, you might want to start with shorter sessions (say, six minutes) and questions on familiar topics—for example, how they feel about various holidays or which movies they like the best. You might also use this opportunity to prompt personal reflection, such as with the following questions: (1) What are your high school and college plans? (2) What do you think your biggest challenges will be? (3) How do you expect to deal with these challenges? Once they've gained their footing, you can shift their attention to more academic topics and texts. The bottom line is this: if you can make everyone as comfortable as possible when launching this challenging task, it could become an invaluable tool in your classroom. Indeed, in one class where I coached the co-teachers, their students began to *request* Socratic Seminars as a way to process what they were learning.

- **Keep in mind that in order to conduct effective discussions about texts, students must read and analyze texts effectively.** Check out Chapter Two, especially the section on During-Reading Strategies such as annotation. Also, the TLC "Analyzing Literature" page has more information on how to teach students how to annotate and analyze texts.

Following are key documents you'll need in order to run Socratic Seminars. These are also found on the TLC "Socratic Seminars" page. The first one is Socratic Seminar Questions on Persuasive Texts (also available on the TLC "Socratic Seminars" page). The second document is Socratic Seminar Questions on Short Stories (also available on the TLC "Socratic Seminars" page), which includes a Note-Taking Form for Audience Members. The third document is a Socratic Seminar Observation Checklist (also available on the TLC "Socratic Seminars" page). The fourth document is a Socratic Seminar Rubric (also available on the TLC "Socratic Seminars" page).

Socratic Seminar Questions on Persuasive Texts[22]

Title of Text _____

The participants will discuss these questions. Audience members will take notes on this handout.

1. What is the main idea or argument?

   _____

   _____

2. What compositional risks does the writer take in trying to prove his or her points?

   _____

   _____

3. What are the most important supporting details?

   _____

   _____

4. What would be the counterarguments to those presented here?

   _____

   _____

5. How successful do you think the writer is in proving his or her argument?

   _____

   _____

6. Do you agree or disagree with the writer? Why? Give *evidence*.

   _____

   _____

7. *For audience members only:* Which participant do you most agree with, and *why?* (Use the back of this page if necessary.)

   _____

   _____

Socratic Seminar Questions on Short Stories[23]

Your group has ten to fifteen minutes to discuss the story. In any order you choose, discuss some or all of the questions below, providing *quotes or paraphrased evidence* from the story to support your arguments. *Note:* Discuss at least *one* question from each category.

Setting

- How important is the setting of the story? Does it really matter? Why or why not?
- How does it contribute to the overall meaning or message?

Tone or Mood

- What is the tone or mood of the story?
- How does the author convey that tone or mood?

Characters

- What inferences can we draw about the characters, based on their actions?
- What major challenges do the characters face, and how do they deal with them?
- What major decisions do the characters make, and why? What do these decisions reveal about the characters?
- Can you relate to any of the characters? If so, explain how.

Symbols or Motifs

- What motifs or symbols recur in the text, and how do they add to the understanding of character, setting, or theme?
- What is the significance of the title, and how does it add to your understanding of the text?

(continued)

Socratic Seminar Questions on Short Stories (*continued*)

Style and Writer's Decisions

- How are sensory details used in this story, and to what effect?
- What passages in the story drew your attention the most, and why?
- What specifically did you like or dislike about this story, and why?
- Does this story remind you of anything else you've read?
- If you were the author, what would you have done differently ("I would not have written this story" is not a sufficiently deep response!)

Point of View

- From whose point of view (POV) do we see the story?
- Why do you think the author chose this POV instead of a different one?
- Compared to other aspects of the story, how important is POV in this story?
- How would the story change if we saw it from a different character's perspective? Pick a different character and explain how the story would change.

Lessons or Messages

- What lessons do the characters learn?
- What lessons do *we* learn?

Name _____ Date _____

Note-Taking Form for Audience Members[24]

In the space below, record your notes on the Socratic Seminar. Use the back if needed.

Story title: _____ **Author:** _____

Setting

_____

_____

_____

Tone or Mood

_____

_____

_____

Characters

_____

_____

_____

Symbols or Motifs

_____

_____

_____

Style and Writer's Decisions

_____

_____

_____

Point of View

_____

_____

_____

Lessons or Messages

_____

_____

_____

Observer _____ Date _____

Socratic Seminar Observation Checklist[25]

Person being observed _____

Check off the description that best applies to your subject's performance in today's Socratic Seminar.

Analysis

How often did the member participate?

❑ Always

❑ Often

❑ Rarely

❑ Never

Did the individual participate voluntarily, or did he or she need to be prompted?

❑ Always participated without prompting

❑ Often participated without prompting

❑ Rarely participated without prompting

❑ Only participated with prompting

❑ Not applicable: the subject did not participate at all

How would you describe the depth of the individual's analysis? (Did he or she infer, make connections, draw conclusions, and make judgments?)

❑ Deep

❑ Solid

❑ Weak

Understanding

Choose the word that best describes the individual's understanding of the text.

❑ Deep

❑ Solid

(continued)

Socratic Seminar Observation Checklist (*continued*)

❑ General

❑ Weak

❑ It's hard to know because the individual rarely participated

Active Listening and Extension

Check off any of the following used by the individual to demonstrate active listening.

❑ Body language (such as eye contact and nodding)

❑ Comments

❑ Questions

How often did the individual extend the conversation with comments or questions that followed up on another member's statements?

❑ Often

❑ Rarely

❑ Never

Evidence

How often did the individual use evidence from the text to support his or her statements?

❑ Always

❑ Often

❑ Rarely: relied more on opinion than text

❑ Never: relied completely on opinion

Comments (please be specific)

_____

_____

_____

_____

Socratic Seminar Rubric[26] **for** _____ **Score** _____

	Outstanding	Satisfactory	Needs Improvement	Unsatisfactory
Analysis	Provides deep analysis, without prompting, to move the conversation forward	Provides solid analysis, without prompting, to move the conversation forward	Offers some analysis, but needs prompting from others	Offers little or no analysis
Understanding	Demonstrates a deep knowledge of the text and the questions	Demonstrates a solid knowledge of the text and the questions	Demonstrates a general knowledge of the text and the questions	Demonstrates a weak knowledge of the text and questions
Preparation	Has come to the seminar prepared, with extensive notes and a heavily marked text	Has come to the seminar prepared, with notes and a marked text	Has come to the seminar inadequately prepared, with few notes and little or no marked text	Has come to the seminar ill-prepared, lacking notes or a marked-up text
Active listening and extension	Shows he or she is actively listening through body language, comments, and questions	Shows he or she is actively listening through body language, comments, and questions	Rarely shows he or she is actively listening through body language	Does not show active listening; body language and posture is unprofessional or inappropriate

(continued)

Socratic Seminar Rubric (continued)

	Outstanding	Satisfactory	Needs Improvement	Unsatisfactory
Active listening and extension (continued)	Offers clarification and/or follow-up that extends the conversation by building on others' comments	Offers some clarification and/or follow-up	Does not offer clarification and/or follow-up to others' comments	Does not offer clarification and/or follow-up to others' comments
Evidence	Almost always refers to specific examples in the text	Often refers to specific examples in the text	Relies more upon his or her opinion, and less on the text to drive his or her comments	Relies almost totally on his or her opinion, and less on the text to drive his or her comments
Fluency and use of standard English	Consistently uses standard English and sophisticated vocabulary; makes few, if any, errors and always self-corrects	Consistently uses standard English; may make occasional errors, but usually self-corrects	Does not consistently use standard English; makes errors and rarely self-corrects	Frequently fails to use standard English; makes frequent errors

BOOK TALK PROJECTS

Growing up, we've probably all sat through endless droning book reports—bored, frustrated, or daydreaming—just waiting for them to be over. The Nonfiction Book Talk Project and Book Talk Project for Class Novel solve this problem. Both projects require—indeed, depend upon—*active* audience participation. Descriptions of both follow.

Here's how the Nonfiction Book Talk Project works: each student reads a nonfiction book, describes it briefly, then answers the audience's questions about it.

This assignment has worked very well with high school students; elementary and middle school teachers have also modified it for their students; and it also works for different genres. In addition to being a more compelling vehicle for oral presentations than the traditional book report—because it engages the entire class and holds audience members accountable for listening, taking notes, and asking questions—the Nonfiction Book Talk Project entices students to read books that their peers have introduced.

Following is an overview of the assignment, which includes the audience's questions, a scoring checklist, and a notes organizer for audience members. The Nonfiction Book Talk Project and a file called Recommended Nonfiction can both be found on the TLC "Book Talk Projects" page.

Name _____ Date _____

Nonfiction Book Talk Project[27]

A. *Prepare a blurb* of one to two minutes. You must include:

Title

Author

Your answer to the question, What is this book about?

   Practice your blurb. *Time it!* It must be within the time frame, or you will lose points if it is too short or too long!

B. For about eight to ten more minutes, members of the studio audience will ask you some of the following questions. You must answer clearly and thoroughly, providing specific evidence that you recall from the book. You may use note cards, but do not flip through the book.

1. Is this book similar to any other book you've read?

2. Did this book change your mind about the topic?

3. Would you recommend this book to others? Why?

4. What adjectives come to mind when you think of this book?

5. What made the author write this book?

6. Why did you choose this book?

7. What was your favorite part?

8. What did you dislike about the book, if anything?

9. Would you read something else by the same author?

10. Would you read something else on the same topic?

(continued)

11. If you hadn't chosen this book, what else would you have chosen, and why (either a specific title or a topic that you are interested in)?

12. What is the author's point of view on the topic?

13. What questions would you ask the author if you could? Why?

14. If this book were made into a movie, who would star in it?

15. What surprised you? Why?

16. What was the most important thing you learned?

17. *Other:* Someone might ask you a relevant question that is not on this list.

Scoring

_____/ 30 points: Blurb timing, completeness, and pacing

_____/ 30: Thoroughness and specificity of responses to questions

_____/ 20: Use of standard English and sophisticated vocabulary

_____/ 10: Eye contact with range of audience members

_____/ 10: Appropriate volume and poise

_____/ **100 points TOTAL**

Audience members will ask questions and take notes on the Book Talk Notes Organizer.

Name _____ Date _____

Book Talk Notes Organizer (for Audience Members)[28]

Presenter _____

Title _____

Author _____

Three things I learned from this presentation:

1.

2.

3.

How much I would like to read this book:

1 _____ 5 _____ 10

No way   **Maybe**   **Definitely**

Explain *why*:

In the Book Talk Project for Class Novel, everyone in the class reads the same novel, but different students take responsibility for different chapters. Depending on the number of chapters to be discussed, students can work alone or in pairs, or you can even incorporate the questions into Socratic Seminars (see the section Socratic Seminars Made Easy earlier in this chapter). Following is an overview of the assignment.

The project includes two simple graphic organizers: (1) The Book Talk for Class Novel Preparation handout helps students organize their ideas logically as they prepare to present, and (2) audience members use the Book Talk for Class Novel Notes handout to take notes. These organizers can be found in the Book Talk Project for Class Novel file on the TLC "Book Talk Projects" page.

Book Talk Project for Class Novel[29]

After students have read the entire book, assign each student a different chapter. Then give these directions.

Each student will give a brief (one- to two-minute) summary of events in his or her assigned chapter. When summarizing fiction, students should consider the following questions:

- *Decisions with purpose.* What major decisions do the characters make, and why?

- *Conflicts, obstacles, or challenges.* What conflicts, obstacles, or challenges do the characters face, and how do they deal with them?

- *Lessons, insights, or messages.* What lessons do any of the characters learn? What do *we* learn?

- *Causes and effects.* What events or actions have major effects on characters? How do the characters react?

- *Patterns.* What patterns from either this passage or the rest of the book do you notice in this passage?

(continued)

(*continued*)

Then, for another five to seven minutes, the audience will ask some or all of the following questions. Presenters must answer clearly and thoroughly, providing specific evidence from the chapter. They may refer to note cards, sticky notes in the chapter, or the Book Talk for Class Novel Preparation handout.

1. How did this chapter change your mind about any of the characters?
2. What adjectives come to mind when you think of this chapter? Explain.
3. What was your favorite part of this chapter? Why?
4. What did you dislike about this chapter, if anything? Why?
5. What questions would you ask the author (either about this chapter or about the book as a whole) if you could? Why?
6. What surprised you in this chapter? Why?
7. What was the most important thing you learned from this chapter? Explain.

Scoring

_____ / 30 points: Blurb timing, completeness, and pacing

_____ / 30: Thoroughness and specificity of responses to questions

_____ / 20: Use of standard English and sophisticated vocabulary

_____ / 10: Eye contact with range of audience members

_____ / 10: Appropriate volume and poise

_____ / **100 points TOTAL**

Note: Presenters can use the Book Talk for Class Novel Preparation handout. *Audience members* will ask questions and take notes on the Book Talk for Class Novel Notes handout.

DOGGIE BAG

1. What do effective Book Talk Projects look like?
2. Which aspects of Book Talk Projects do you think your students might struggle with, and how will you set them up for success?

TLC DOWNLOADS FOR SPEAKING AND LISTENING

Socratic Seminar Questions on Persuasive Texts

Socratic Seminar Questions on Short Stories

Book Talk Project for Class Novel

Socratic Seminar Observation Checklist

Socratic Seminar Rubric

Recommended Nonfiction

Nonfiction Book Talk Project

Entrées

Now that we've taken some time to absorb the basic ingredients of effective literacy instruction, we can explore compelling ways to combine them. The purpose of the Entrées chapters is to provide practical guidance on how to set students up for success on assessments that involve a mixture of reading, writing, speaking, and listening.

In this section, we'll focus on the following items:

- Tasty Persuasive Writing
- Reading, Writing, and Test Prep "Stew"
- The Document-Based Question Approach
- Research Paper Guide
- Teaching with Novels

Bon appetit!

Tasty Persuasive Writing

THE CONCEPT OF PERSUASION

Virtually every form of writing includes some element of persuasion—whether overtly in an op-ed piece or subliminally in a poem. Whenever we write, we are trying to convey a message or an argument: we want to make people feel, think, or believe something. This is why it's so important for students to understand the concept of persuasion: it's not just in letters to the editor, it's everywhere.

Some people think that the best way to win an argument is to steamroll the other side with their ideas. But that doesn't really work (possibly because most people don't appreciate being crushed). For something to be persuasive, it has to be tasty. Even if it expresses an idea that I as the reader wouldn't normally agree with, it has to include something compelling and make me believe that one of my arguments isn't as strong as I originally thought.

When teaching students to write persuasively, we must remind them that it's not enough to prove you are right; you must also prove that the opposition is wrong or its arguments are weaker. Simply listing all of the arguments and facts that support your views is not appealing or sufficient, which is why attorneys don't rely on that approach. They find ways to disprove the other side's arguments. One way is to include the Straw Man. Contrary to what some might think, he's not "some guy with a sippy straw," as one student speculated when I asked if the class had ever heard of him before. As I like to tell students, he's "an idea from the other side that you set up so you can knock him down." I like to pretend I'm swinging a bat when I say this.

Empathy is important to persuasion. In *They Say/I Say*, Gerald Graff and Cathy Birkenstein demonstrate how academic writing requires that you summarize what others believe in order to set up your own argument; they refer to this "they say/I say" template as "the internal DNA of all effective argument."[1] Indeed, this approach works well not just for explicitly persuasive writing but for any academic writing in which an argument is to be proven. If you look back at the second paragraph in this chapter, for example, you'll see that I used this technique myself.

Once students grasp the concept of persuasion, you can drill down into particular moves that are effective. As noted in the section on Teaching with Mentor Texts in Chapter Three, it's important to show examples of what you're looking for, and Graff and Birkenstein provide numerous explicit examples of how to begin, develop, and conclude persuasive pieces of writing, including templates and sentence starters to illustrate moves that effective writers make, such as "Many people assume that _____," and "While they rarely admit as much, _____ often take for granted that _____."[2] Students need to know that persuasion is not magic; it's systematic.

HOW TO PREPARE STUDENTS FOR PERSUASIVE WRITING TASKS

Many standardized tests require students to respond to a prompt by writing a persuasive letter or essay. Here is a simple recipe:

1. **Make sure students understand the concept of *persuasion*.** In particular, they need to know that it is not simply making a list of reasons why you're right but also explaining why the other side is wrong. Lawyers and debaters have to understand both sides of an argument in order to win.

2. **Give students examples of effective persuasive writing to read, analyze, and discuss.** They can practice their oral argument skills in Socratic Seminars (see Chapter Four).

3. **As with every writing task, give students models to critique.** Most states that require persuasive writing on their standardized tests provide scored exemplars for this purpose.

4. **Point out "compositional risks" such as rhetorical questions, strong vocabulary, and irony, and keep a running list on a poster as the class encounters them.**[3]

5. **Require students to *practice prewriting* many times.** Prewriting should include these steps: (1) annotate the task to clarify what you need to know and do (typically this involves looking for "PAT"—Policy or Problem, Audience, and Task); (2) create a T-chart of arguments for both sides, pick the side you will defend, and circle one argument from the other side that you will knock down (the Straw Man); and (3) use a Persuasive Writing Task Organizer (see next; variations are also available on the TLC "NJ ASK Prep" and "NJ HSPA Prep" pages) to outline your letter or essay.

6. **Give timely feedback on the actual writing.** As noted in Chapter Three's "A Simple Recipe for Writing Instruction," if they can't figure out how to fix *this* essay, how can we expect them to do better on the next one?

Persuasive Writing Task Organizer[4]

Salutation (if it's a letter):

Dear _____:

Introduction. Explain why you are writing.

- What is your role in the school or community?
- What new policy has been proposed, and by whom?
- Why do you think they proposed this policy?
- Do you *support* or *oppose* this policy?

Body 1. Explain one reason why you support or oppose this policy.

  Note: When you write the paragraph, give vivid specific details to support this reason.

Body 2. Explain another reason why you support or oppose this policy.

  Note: When you write the paragraph, give vivid specific details to support this reason.

Body 3. Explain another reason why you support or oppose this policy.

(*continued*)

(continued)

> *Note:* When you write the paragraph, give vivid specific details to support this reason.

Body 4. Set up the "Straw Man" and knock him down.

- What is one argument the opposing side could make? Tell what's wrong with it.
- *Conclusion.* Tell what you think the reader or audience should do. *Either* they should go ahead with the policy *or* they should not. If *not*, tell them respectfully what they should do *instead*.

Closing:

Sincerely,

Your Name

DOGGIE BAG

1. What do students need to know about the concept of persuasion?

2. What are the key steps for effective persuasive writing?

3. What aspects of persuasive writing do you think your students might struggle with, and how will you set them up for success?

Reading, Writing, and Test Prep "Stew"

AN ARGUMENT FOR STEW

Anyone who has eaten cooked carrots, potatoes, or beef alone on a plate knows that a little bit goes a long way, but when you put these ingredients together in a pot, something magical happens and you find yourself going back for seconds. Similarly, as wonderful as reading, writing, and test preparation might be on their own, they are more delicious when combined.

Some people believe that the field of education has become too focused on test preparation. I taught for seven years before the No Child Left Behind Act passed and for another seven years after that. While I have seen some schools going overboard with test preparation, I've also observed one undeniably positive impact: people are paying more attention to the performance of struggling schools and the students in them. They have seen the data on the Achievement Gap and are trying to close it. Whereas in the past mostly fourth- and eighth-grade teachers worried about test scores, now virtually all teachers in grades 3–8 are aware of how their students are doing. Also, school leaders in low-performing districts have begun to rethink their old policies of social promotion, realiz-

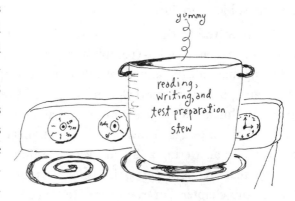

ing, for example, *Students who can't read won't be able to pass the tests, so we'd better teach these kids how to read*. To which I say, *Good idea*.

That said, while it's important to prepare students to pass tests, it's also important to develop their love of reading, writing, and learning. And the good news is that you *can* do all of these things. That's what this chapter is about.

CONNECTING KEY CRITICAL READING SKILLS TO TEST PREP INSTRUCTION

In order to read effectively, students must understand the Comprehension Process and how to paraphrase, infer, draw meaning from vocabulary in context, and infer the main idea or argument. Coincidentally, when taking reading tests, they need these same skills. So here is my proposition: teach them the skills directly, teach them the testing code words (which reveal the skill being tested—more on this in a moment), teach them basic test-taking strategies, and then give them lots of practice in applying the key critical reading skills to whatever texts you choose. They don't have to "do test prep" every day in order to pass standardized tests. They *do* need to learn how to read well.

Now, let's take a closer look at the first three steps.

1. **Teach the Comprehension Process and the four key critical reading skills directly.** Chapter One explains how to do this. If you can convince all of your colleagues to join you on this quest, the results in every subject area will be amazing. PS: I am not speculating. I have worked with schools that have actually done this, applying a "full-court press" of paraphrasing and inference instruction in every class in the first few weeks of school (and beyond). It sends a powerful message to students—that critical reading skills can help you comprehend texts in *every* subject, not just in English.

2. **Teach the testing code words.** If students can determine what type of question is being asked (paraphrasing, inference, vocabulary in context, or inferring main idea or argument), then they can apply the appropriate skill. And they can apply their knowledge of the genre of reading tests to great effect. For example, "main idea" questions require an argument (if it's about a nonfiction passage) or a message or theme (if it's a fictional or narrative passage), *not a fact*. So if you're answering a "main idea" question, you can eliminate any answer choices that are facts. This point is demonstrated in the Test Prep Tips section later in this chapter. For examples of testing code words, see the section on How to Design Critical Reading Questions next.

3. **Teach basic test-taking strategies.** Although the adults in the building are all familiar with standardized tests and strategies like using the process of elimination, it's a mistake to assume that our students possess such basic test-taking savvy. Tests are a genre; once students know the conventions of this genre, they will be able to comprehend tests more easily. See the Test Prep Tips section later in this chapter.

Design Good Critical Reading Questions

Even though you shouldn't spend every day on test prep, it helps to know how to design critical reading questions so that you can weave them into your instruction, assignments, and assessments. Following is a recipe (found on the TLC "Connecting Reading, Writing, and Test Prep" page) that you can use with virtually any passage.

First, read the passage. As you read, identify at least two Tier 2 vocabulary words[1] (words they don't know but should be able to figure out from context, especially words that are essential to understanding the passage; avoid jargon) and determine the *main idea or argument*. Note where you have to answer the question *Why?* so you can come back and create *inference* questions based on these sections.

Then follow the guidance offered next to write your questions.

Critical Reading Skills and How to Design Their Questions	Sample Questions

Paraphrasing *Find two sections with material that students can paraphrase, and create two paraphrasing or literal comprehension questions.*
• *Note:* You can paraphrase the stem *or* the answer choices.
• Try to focus on sections of the text that are *essential* to understanding the passage, not extraneous details that happen to be written in a complicated way.
	1. Which of the following factors significantly hindered the firefighters?
	  A. They didn't have enough water.
	  B. They had lost their chief.
	  C. Transportation was difficult because the streets were damaged.
	  D. All of the above.
	
	2. How did the family determine that Oliver was blind?
	  A. The doctor at the hospital told them Oliver was blind.

(continued)

Critical Reading Skills and How to Design Their Questions	Sample Questions
• Do not ask students to translate arcane jargon or terminology. • Do not use verbatim language from the text as a correct answer choice. In other words, students should not simply skim to find the exact wording of the right answer. No Where's Waldo questions! **Code words** for the question stem: • Facts • In other words • According to the story or passage • What does this mean? • Plot • Paraphrase	B. Oliver's eyes did not react to bright sunlight. C. Oliver was blind from birth. D. The test at Mt. Sinai hospital confirmed that Oliver had a terrible disease. 3. "But then they always awoke to the tatting drum, the endless shaking down of clear bead necklaces upon the roof, the walk, the gardens, the forest, and their dreams were gone." This passage refers to: A. the rain B. the noisy neighborhood C. the sound of the TV D. their alarm clocks
Inference *Find two sections where you had to infer, and create two inference questions.* **Code words** for the question stem: • Infer • Suggest • Conclude • Because or why • Most likely • Probably	1. The two men were probably attempting to: A. escape to Mexico. B. find a bank to rob. C. visit someone in Hackett. D. hide their stolen car. 2. Why do the animals walk right by Tiger when he is hunting? A. They do not see Tiger. B. They are not afraid of Tiger. C. They know Tiger will not eat them. D. Tiger tells them to play at that time.

Critical Reading Skills and How to Design Their Questions	Sample Questions
	3. What can you infer about the first woman the narrator brought home? A. She wanted to help cook dinner. B. She had already met Oliver before. C. She wanted to spend more time with his parents. D. He broke up with her because she was insensitive.
Vocabulary in Context *Identify two Tier 2 vocabulary words, and create two vocabulary in context (VIC) questions. Be sure to include a* distractor *that uses a different definition of the word.* • Other wrong answers can sound like the word itself or like a plausible definition (just not the definition that fits in this particular context). • Make sure the sentences you choose provide sufficient context. These are not just vocabulary questions; they are vocabulary *in context* questions. **Code words** for the question stem: • What does _____ mean in this context? • Based on the passage, what does _____ mean?	1. "He got their coffee first, then started *rooting* through a pile of papers by the telephone, looking for a map." In this context, *rooting* means A. cheering for B. stretching C. turning D. digging 2. "One person in every three would die of the plague before it *ran its course*." In this context, the expression *ran its course* means A. ran in circles B. began to occur C. came to an end D. spread to Europe 3. "So many people were struck down by the plague that the supply of coffins was soon *exhausted*, and the dead were carried

(continued)

Critical Reading Skills and How to Design Their Questions	Sample Questions
	on wooden planks to huge mass-burial pits." In this context, *exhausted* means A. very tired B. hopeless C. thin D. used up
Finding the Main Idea or Argument *State the main idea (MI) or argument. This becomes the correct answer for your MI question (such as "What is the main idea of this passage?" or "This passage is mainly about . . .").* *Then create an MI question with four responses (one correct). Make three wrong answers for the MI question. Here are some options:* • Something true but not the main idea • Something mentioned early in the passage but not the main idea • Something that is a *fact*, not an argument • Something that seems like it could be the main idea but isn't • Something too broad to be the main idea • Something too specific to be the main idea	1. Which of the following is the main idea of this passage? A. Earthquakes and fires can be a deadly combination. B. Broken power and gas lines set off fires throughout San Francisco in 1906. C. The tremors from the San Francisco earthquake in 1906 destroyed 38,000 buildings. D. The San Francisco earthquake and the fires it caused were responsible for death and destruction in 1906. 2. Which of the following statements best expresses the theme of the story? A. One should never eat at an unfamiliar place. B. You can't always judge what a person is like by a first impression. C. It isn't wise to be helpful to strangers. D. You should never trust strangers.

Critical Reading Skills and How to Design Their Questions	Sample Questions
Code words for the question stem: • After reading the article, passage, or story . . . • The central idea or the main idea • The theme • This passage is mostly about • The author would probably agree • The best summary	3. The main idea of this passage is: A. The yearly festival in Pamplona, Spain, always includes the Running of the Bulls. B. Running alongside the bulls as they are moved from the corral to the bullring in Pamplona, Spain, has become an exciting and dangerous sport. C. The bravest runners carry newspapers with which they touch the bulls as they run through the streets. D. The Running of the Bulls in Pamplona, Spain, has been going on for about three hundred years.

TEST PREP TIPS

The following test prep tips are also available on the TLC "Generic Test Prep Strategies" page.

General Tip 1. Just because it's true, that doesn't mean it's the right answer. It has to be the *best* answer. Read all choices carefully.

General Tip 2. Use POE (Process of Elimination) and be sure you can explain why wrong answers are wrong. (*Hint to teachers:* For practice, provide lines next to each answer so that students can explain why the wrong answers are wrong.)

General Tip 3. It's helpful if you have background knowledge when you're reading a passage, but don't let that drown out the text. Sometimes test passages include information that you might not have known.

Example

According to the passage, most sharks are . . .

A. Smaller than most people realize

B. Larger than most people realize

C. Dangerous to humans

D. Larger than five feet long

A is actually the correct answer, although most people who haven't read the passage would probably guess C.

General Tip 4. When answering questions, go back into the text and write the number of the question you're answering next to the paragraph where it is addressed. Read the whole paragraph and use the context in answering the question. You will be amazed at how much your results improve!

General Tip 5. **Do not rush.** Students who rush because they think they are "so smart" often get more questions wrong than students who work hard, take their time, and check their work. Test makers create distractors specifically intended to trick students who rush. In *Driven by Data*, Paul Bambrick-Santoyo includes the Williamsburg Collegiate Student Assessment Reflection Template, which enables students to reflect upon their performance to determine if they are exhibiting the traits of Rushing Roger or Backseat Betty so that they can learn from their mistakes.[2]

Main Idea Tips

1. For the main idea you selected, you should be able to give two to three pieces of evidence to support it (three bullet points). If you can't find the evidence, it's probably not the main idea or argument.

2. In *fiction* or *narratives*, the main idea should be a *message* that revolves around the main character. Answer choices that focus on minor characters can probably be eliminated.

3. If the question asks for the main idea of a *nonfiction passage*, the answer should be *an argument, not a fact.*

Example

The main idea of this passage is:

A. The yearly festival in Pamplona, Spain, always includes the Running of the Bulls. (*fact*)

B. Running alongside the bulls as they are moved from the corral to the bullring in Pamplona, Spain, has become an exciting and dangerous sport. (The words *exciting* and *dangerous* are debatable or arguable, requiring evidence and explanation; therefore, this is an *argument*.)

C. The bravest runners carry newspapers with which they touch the bulls as they run through the streets. (*factish* and *too specific*)

D. The Running of the Bulls in Pamplona, Spain, has been going on for about three hundred years. (*fact*)

Vocabulary in Context Tips

1. Use *cloze* reading first. Don't even look at the answer choices! Look at the sentence and circle *clues* that suggest meaning. Fill in the blank with your own idea. *Then* compare your idea to the answer choices.

Example

In the sentence, "Police had to *divert* traffic because of the overturned tractor trailer," what does *divert* mean?

A. Amuse

B. Distract

C. Change the route of

D. Speed up

2. *Read the whole paragraph*, not just the sentence that the vocabulary word appears in. That's why they're called *in context*. If you don't read the context, you will rely on the most common usage of the word, which 90 percent of the time is the distractor (that is, the wrong answer that people select because it's how they always think of the word). Test makers are sneaky, but in a predictable way. Vocabulary *in context* questions are not merely *vocabulary* questions. They require you to attend to the *context.* The answer choices typically include a distractor "synonym" that uses the target word in a context different from the one on the test. (For example, *divert* means *amuse* in one context and *change the route* in another. Some students who are rushing and think they're "so smart" might guess *amuse* and get this one wrong.)

Example

In paragraph 2, the word *alert* means:

- **A.** Wide awake
- **B.** Trick
- **C.** Surprise
- **D.** Warn

If you didn't read the paragraph and just relied on the typical usage of *alert* as *wide awake*, you would get this question wrong. In this instance, *alert* was used as a verb meaning *warn*.

Why It Helps to Triangulate

It's important to collect multiple data points when making decisions about instruction. This lesson was brought home to me while analyzing the results of a quarterly literacy assessment with several third-grade teachers.

As we pored over the results around a table in the principal's office, one teacher expressed shock at how poorly some of the students had done. "Samantha [not her real name] is one of our top readers, and she totally bombed the test! And that's true for a few others!" She pointed to a chart on the wall, which showed another set of data: students' WRAP (Writing and Reading Assessment Profile) results. According to the WRAP, Samantha was actually reading on the fifth-grade level. "And I know this is true," said the teacher, "because I've seen the books she's reading."

The teacher recalled that several students had finished early. "I think they just rushed," she concluded. "They seem to think that if they finish first, it means they're smart," she added. "It drives me crazy."

Someone in their orbit must have been praising speed.

We came up with this solution: she would go over the test with her students and direct them to star any questions they thought they could've gotten correct if they had taken more time. She could then point out how many points they'd lost as a result of their haste. Let them draw their own conclusions.

A few days later, I saw this teacher and asked her how it went.

"Were they remorseful?" I asked.

"Absolutely. They totally got the point," she replied. "Lesson learned."

And a lesson for us all: triangulate. One data point is not enough. If we hadn't known the students' reading levels, we might have assumed that they had failed because they were weak readers.

And another thing: be careful what you praise.

DOGGIE BAG

1. How can you *efficiently* prepare your students to do better on reading tests?

2. What does it take to design effective critical reading questions?

3. Which test prep tips will you teach your students?

CONNECTING WRITING TO READING THROUGH GENRE STUDY

As a high school English teacher for fourteen years, I was always baffled by elementary and middle school teachers who told me that they taught "language arts" and "writing" (and sometimes "reading") separately. "What's language arts?" I would ask. I'm not sure anyone ever answered that question either the same way or to my satisfaction. Then I would ask, "And why are those things separated?" Again, I'm still wondering. I think in some schools, the principals wanted to make sure that both reading and writing were covered, so they labeled them and assigned different people to teach them. All I know for sure is that the thought of teaching reading and writing apart from each other feels like a missed opportunity.

As noted repeatedly throughout this book, students need to see models of the excellent writing that we expect them to produce. While you can certainly do this in a piecemeal way, a more coherent approach to consider is *genre study*. In *Thinking Through Genre*, Heather Lattimer presents a half dozen case studies to explain and illustrate how to integrate reading and writing workshops so that students learn the main characteristics of a genre, then apply that knowledge by writing in that genre.[3] In short, students read first to understand the genre, then they write in that genre.

What I love about genre study is its clear sense of purpose. It's not just a bunch of randomly grabbed passages, or worse, the next thing that appears in the textbook. Notice the contrast between "Everybody turn to page 85" and "Today we're going to begin reading and analyzing editorials so that we can learn how to write them."

In addition to being logical, genre study is meaningful and practical. As Lattimer notes, students must tackle some meaty questions: "What makes this genre unique? What do we need to know and be able to do in order to be successful readers of this genre?" And the connection between reading and writing is made plain: "What language and structures do successful writers of this genre use, and how can that inform our own writing?"[4] Students are not merely observers or describers of a genre: as they read like writers, then write for readers, they begin to *own* the genre.

Now, I can hear people saying, "If genre study is so great, why don't people do it all the time?" Good question. For one thing, it sounds simpler than it is. You need training in how to run reading and writing workshops or at least one of them before you attempt to interweave them. You must also be highly observant and flexible. Lattimer notes that while you can map out a rough schedule for the unit, the specifics such as "individual mini-lessons, discussion prompts, and workshop expectations are typically planned on a week-to-week or day-to-day basis. So much depends on what is observed about student learning—how students react to a particular text, how they apply (or fail to apply) a strategy, what else is going on in their reading and writing."[5] Teaching with this method requires a high tolerance for ambiguity, plus solid organizational skills.

Another factor to consider before launching genre study is, of course, how it fits into your curriculum. Now that many schools and districts have begun to revise curriculum as a result of adopting the Common Core Standards, teachers have an opportunity to identify more purposeful text selections and attach them to writing objectives. (PS: For more information on the Common Core State Standards, see http://www.corestandards.org. Also, check out the TLC "Standards" page for the K–12 ELA Common Core Standards Tracking Sheet, which lists each grade's standards on a separate spreadsheet. A snippet of this document, which is particularly handy when writing or evaluating curriculum, appears in the Appendix of this book.)

In sum, it's not easy, but it can be done. My suggestion is to read Lattimer's book, attend training on how to conduct either reading or writing workshops (or, even better, both), and map out a pilot unit. If you can involve one or more of your colleagues in the mix, that would help. Having someone to bounce ideas off of—and an extra set of eyes to monitor how things are going—can make it easier for you to keep track of what you and the students are learning.

DOGGIE BAG

1. What is genre study, and how does it work?
2. Which aspects of genre study might you incorporate in your classroom?

OPEN-ENDED RESPONSES

Although not a huge fan of standardized tests, I am thankful to whoever designed the NJ ASK (New Jersey Assessment of Skills and Knowledge) tests for one thing: the open-ended response questions. It's weird, I know, but they gave me some insight. So to speak.

Here's what happened: I was working with a bunch of schools that wanted to improve their students' scores on the NJ ASK, and we were trying to figure out what it would take to earn a 4 out of 4 on the open-ended response questions. The state's rubric was no help; for example, none of us were really sure what "clearly demonstrates understanding of the task" meant. So I studied the state-released sample questions and exemplars, and eventually I was able to crack the code and create a more concrete, user-friendly rubric (which follows shortly).

Here is what I noticed: the questions all required inference and used this stock epithet: "Use specific information from the passage and any additional insight to support your response." The highest-scoring exemplars ended with punchy insights. They weren't dull, "here's-what-I-just-told-you" conclusions; they actually provided a spark of a message, some bit of wisdom.

It occurred to me that we could teach our students to write these punchy insights. In fact, we needed to, because that's what writing is all about: conveying a message and making an impact with words. So I created the Punchy Insights Poster. To avoid repeating myself and save a few trees, let me refer you back to the section called Punchy Insights, or How to Avoid Writing Like a Robot, in Chapter Three. It includes the poster and a full explanation of how to teach about insights.

Even if your students are not taking the NJ ASK (or NJ HSPA, which also requires open-ended responses), I suspect you will find the following rubric (also found on the TLC "Writing Rubrics" page) helpful for any inference-based, open-ended response writing.

OPEN-ENDED RESPONSE RUBRIC[6]

---

4 *Restates* the question, using *names* instead of pronouns.
Answers *all parts* of the question, giving *four to six sentences* per question part.
Provides an insightful explanation using *ample, accurate, and relevant evidence* from the text and your own ideas to support your argument.
Ends with a *punchy statement or insight.*
Uses effective transitions for smooth flow.
Uses strong vocabulary.
No errors in mechanics or usage.

---

3 *Restates* the question.
Answers *all parts* of the question, giving *three to four sentences* per question part.
Provides an explanation using *accurate, relevant evidence* from the text and your own ideas to support your argument.
Ends with *some insight.*
Uses transitions.
Uses some strong vocabulary.
Few errors in mechanics or usage.

(*continued*)

Open-Ended Response Rubric (*continued*)

2   May not *restate* the question.

       May not answer *all parts* of the question, giving only *two to three sentences* per question.

       Provides a weak or incoherent explanation using *skimpy, inaccurate, or irrelevant evidence.*

       Ending is repetitious or weak.

       No transitions, choppy.

       Uses weak vocabulary.

       Many errors in mechanics or usage.

1   Does not *restate* the question.

       Does not answer *all parts* of the question, giving *zero to two sentences* per question.

       Fails to provide *evidence* from the text or your own ideas to support your argument.

       Ending is repetitious, weak, or missing.

       Many errors in mechanics or usage.

As with any rubric, it's important to ensure that students understand all of the terms included—not just what they mean, but also what purposes they serve. What does *ample* evidence look like? Why does evidence need to be *relevant*? How do effective transitions help the flow of our writing? Explaining this rubric could take several mini-lessons. And that would be time well spent.

DOGGIE BAG

1. What does an effective open-ended writing response look like?

2. Why are "punchy insights" important, and how can we teach them?

The Document-Based Question Approach

WHAT ARE DBQs, AND WHY SHOULD EVERYONE USE THEM?

Most people who have heard of DBQs (Document-Based Questions) associate them with history or social studies teachers, because they appear on AP history exams and New York State Regents social studies exams. Those DBQs look like this:

- A handful of "texts," such as photos, political cartoons, charts, graphs, articles, speeches, and letters

- A bit of background information (usually a brief paragraph of historical context)

- One to three questions

- A description of the task

Students must write a well-organized essay using evidence from the documents, including relevant facts, examples, and details, plus additional outside information.

Although DBQs have been limited primarily to the domain of history and social studies, I believe teachers of *every* subject can use the DBQ Approach as an efficient vehicle for teaching both content and critical thinking skills.

The DBQ Approach, put simply, is as follows: select an open-ended question (or more than one, if you prefer) that you want students to respond to (see suggestions in the next section). Give them multiple relevant "texts" to interpret and employ in response to this question. Students must then build an *argument* using the documents as *evidence*. Sound familiar?

Indeed, DBQ essays require many of the skills involved in writing a research paper: close reading and analysis, inference, summarizing, and synthesizing ideas. But in this case, the teacher provides the research and the driving question(s). So DBQ essays are like research papers with training wheels, or "add-water-and-stir" research papers.

Teachers of *any* grade can take the DBQ Approach. Because you control the question(s) and the documents, you determine the difficulty of the assignment. For history and social studies teachers, hundreds or perhaps thousands of sample DBQs are available online. You can find links to numerous such resources on the TLC "History Writing: DBQ Essays" page.[1] The following section offers suggestions for how to apply this approach in other content areas.

DESIGNING DBQs ACROSS THE CURRICULUM

No matter what grade or subject you teach, the most effective springboards for diving into DBQs are essential questions—questions that Wiggins and McTighe note "are not answerable with finality in a brief sentence—and that's the point." Essential questions are meant "to stimulate thought, to provoke inquiry, and to spark more questions."[2] They address the core concepts or issues in a topic, domain, or field, and they push us to think more deeply. For that reason, they are particularly well suited to DBQs, because to answer them, we must build substantial arguments with evidence. Following are some angles to consider:

- If you teach high school English, you might ask, "How does power or the desire for power influence any of the following: (1) the whole society, (2) how individuals behave, or (3) family relationships?" Students could be given a mixture of texts (stories, articles, poems, perhaps even a novel or a play) on which to base their arguments. (PS: You can modify the DBQ Approach to meet your goals and objectives. It does not necessarily have to be a timed essay test based on short texts.)

- Elementary or middle school English teachers might ask, "What makes someone a good friend?" or, "Why is family important?" and offer a handful of poems, stories, and articles.

- Health or physical education teachers could ask, "What is good health?" or, "Why is _____ bad for you?" or, "Why is _____ good for you?" and provide a set of articles, charts, and graphs.

- Science teachers could raise questions about controversial topics such as population growth, climate change, or the environmental impacts of a particular form of energy; again, articles, charts, and graphs would be appropriate, and there might be relevant governmental reports or testimony from public hearings, as well.

Once you've decided on the question(s) and materials, it's vital, as always, to model the skills that students will need in order to complete the DBQ essay successfully. That means paraphrasing, questioning, inferring, and summarizing, for starters. After students have analyzed each text, they will need to synthesize relevant supporting evidence into a coherent argument. The next chapter, on full-blown research papers, takes a more in-depth look at how to support students through this writing process.

DOGGIE BAG

1. What are DBQs, and why should everyone use them?
2. What skills do DBQs require students to practice?
3. What would a DBQ assignment look like in your class?

Research Paper Guide

READING AND THE RESEARCH PAPER

As the previous chapter illustrated, the DBQ Approach is like a research paper with training wheels. Now we're going to explore what happens when you remove the training wheels.

One of my lowest moments as a teacher came the day I collected a set of research papers that my students had been working on for more than a month. They were, quite simply, dreadful. They had thesis statements and quotes and properly cited sources. But their arguments made no sense. The problem wasn't what I had taught. It was what I'd *assumed* they already knew—that they could read documents and pull out the most important arguments and evidence.

"removing the training wheels"

To write *an effective research paper, you must be able to* read *critically*. It may sound simple, but it's not. Here are the *reading-related* steps:

1. Review resources in order to determine a potential topic and relevant arguments.

2. Develop questions about the potential topic and arguments.

3. Locate sources relevant to the selected topic and arguments; evaluate sources for their bias or legitimacy.

4. Read and analyze sources to determine which passages provide compelling, appropriate evidence for your arguments. *This is one of the most challenging steps, and it requires* instruction!

5. Organize and analyze selected evidence to determine whether you have enough evidence to support your arguments. *This requires synthesizing information and ideas—also a difficult step requiring instruction.*

6. Find additional evidence (reviewing existing sources and reading additional sources if needed) and decide if you need to revise your arguments.

7. Reorganize arguments and evidence, analyzing materials to determine whether you can prove your thesis. *Lather, rinse, repeat.*

And that's all before you *write* anything other than note cards and an outline! Bottom line: the biggest mistake we make when teaching the research paper is assuming that students know how to process what they read in the course of doing research.

HOW TO AVOID RPT (RESEARCH PAPER TORTURE)

Probably the second-biggest mistake we make when assigning research papers is that *we fail to frame the work in a way that makes it meaningful and engaging for students.* In other words, we subject the students and ourselves to RPT (Research Paper Torture). The research paper wouldn't seem so scary and/or boring if students were invited to explore a topic that they genuinely cared about. But telling them to "write about anything you want" is not the best solution, either. That could result in papers on skateboarding. Not that there's anything wrong with skateboarding. It just doesn't lend itself to much controversy or to research that builds an argument supported with evidence. Like many randomly-selected topics, it tends to point to the creation of a dull report, with facts cut and pasted into something resembling a multi-page list. Not to mention the plagiarism that goes along with it.

Selecting an appropriate topic is a skill in itself, one we should not overlook.

One way to hook middle and high school students is to cover a table with high-interest nonfiction books and ask students to select one that appeals to them. They don't necessarily have to read the book, though they might decide to. Give them a few minutes to figure out what the book is about (maybe ask them to jot a sentence or two about what they think it's about), then ask them to generate ten to twenty questions about anything relating to the book, including as many *why* and *how* questions as possible, because these will lead to additional exploration.

Most *why* questions will provoke an argument or at least a hypothesis to be tested. For example: "Why did the influenza of 1918 spread so rapidly?" might lead to a theory that people didn't want to enforce quarantines because they could cause panic.

The next section outlines two additional approaches that have proven effective.

TWO SAMPLE RESEARCH PAPER ASSIGNMENTS

The first sample is an Empathy Research Paper assignment. The second sample is a Career Problem-Solving Research Project. Both are also available on the TLC "Research Paper Guide" page.

Sample 1

1. Identify a person (*not* a living celebrity and maybe not even a specific individual) whose shoes you would like to wear for a month in order to understand this person's life situation more fully.

   For example, you might choose:

   • Someone living in Haiti post-earthquake

   • Someone living in Japan post-tsunami

   • Someone living in Alaska or another state that you would like to know more about

   • Someone living in Greece (or another country that has had severe economic troubles)

   Or you might choose someone *not currently living*, but a historical figure or someone in a historical situation—say, if you always wanted to be Thomas Jefferson, Cleopatra, Julius Caesar, Malcolm X, Dr. Martin Luther King Jr., Rosa Parks, or Albert Einstein.

2. Before you begin, write a rationale paragraph (six to eight sentences) about why you are choosing to study this particular person.

3. Write a five- to seven-page research paper answering at least the following questions and any others you want to pursue:

   • Why would you want to be this person? What do you hope to learn?

   (continued)

(continued)

- What problems or challenges does this person face? How is this person trying to solve them?
- How did his or her childhood shape him or her?
- What would a typical day be like in this person's life (judging by your research)?

Note

- If you choose a person who is not living, you must honor the facts of the person's life; you cannot alter history. In other words, you can't warn MLK not to stand outside at the Lorraine Motel.
- You must include an average of two citations per page (minimum ten different sources total, at least two from books) with in-text citations and a Works Cited page using MLA format.
- The Works Cited page does not count toward your five to seven pages.

Sample 2

The basic premise behind the Career Problem-Solving Research Project is that people who love their jobs spend most of their time solving problems that they care deeply about. Students confront these questions: *What job would you like to do? What kinds of problems would you like to solve? If you could learn more about these problems, what kinds of questions would you like to explore?*

In order to clarify their own career interests, students complete a simple survey on the Sixteen Career Clusters. Here's a link to one that has been mimicked on many Websites: http://breitlinks.com/careers/career_pdfs/InterestSurvey.pdf

Timing: ten to fifteen minutes to take it, plus another five to ten minutes to add up the results and read about the clusters.

Students select a cluster, narrow it to a particular career, and brainstorm on problems that someone with this career might be trying to solve. Then

(continued)

(continued)

they think of questions that arise related to these problems (which could be quite divergent, and that's fine).

Here's an example based on the occupation of meteorology:

Problem

One problem for meteorologists is that even though the weather is somewhat predictable, it can also be quite dangerous.

Questions

- Why are we having so many tornadoes these days?
- Why did it snow in October this year?
- Why did the Mississippi River flood so severely recently?
- What factors determine the length and intensity of the hurricane season? Why do we usually have hurricanes at particular times of the year?

Assignment

- Write a three- to four-page research paper that builds an argument about a problem related to a career you might want to pursue.
- The argument should answer a *why* question—such as, Why are we having so many tornadoes these days? Why did the Mississippi River flood so severely recently? Why did the people in Egypt revolt? Why are we still fighting a war in Afghanistan? Why are there so many gangs in cities? Why is unemployment so high for particular demographic groups? Why do people become teachers?
- The paper should use at least *four* different sources, which might include books, newspaper or magazine articles, personal interviews, surveys involving at least twenty-five people, Web pages (but note that Wikipedia is not considered a reliable source), and you must cite sources using MLA format and include a Works Cited page (which doesn't count toward your three to four pages).

(continued)

(continued)

Here are some suggestions about pacing this project with middle school students:

Day 1

- Introduce and explain the goals and objectives of the project.
- Students take and score the Sixteen Clusters Career Survey (see link given earlier).
- Teacher models brainstorming on problems related to a career and questions that follow from these problems.
- Students do their own brainstorming and question generating.

Day 2

- *Mini-lesson:* How to improve your questions (see the TLC "Research Paper Guide" page, which includes two different lists of questions, one effective, one ineffective).
- Spend at least forty-five minutes helping students to refine their twenty questions (which, unlike those in the game Twenty Questions, should be open-ended, not yes-or-no). By the end of the day, they should have a solid list of questions they want to explore.

Day 3

- *Mini-lesson:* How to evaluate sources (see the TLC "Research Paper Guide" page for materials on this). Ask students to evaluate a few random sources that you've selected (from both biased and relatively unbiased sources).
- Give students more time to find their own online resources: ideally two to three more.

Day 4

- *Mini-lesson:* Model how to annotate a source based on the question(s) you're trying to answer.

(continued)

(*continued*)

- Demonstrate how to create *evidence cards* and *source cards* (see the TLC "Research Paper Guide" page). Give students time to annotate, then create evidence and source cards for the sources they've collected so far. *Note:* This project will very quickly require lots of differentiated instruction as students will have different topics, different resources, and different challenges.

Day 5

- Conduct a mini-lesson on organizing evidence cards *as you go*. That way you can see where you have enough information and where you have holes. Students should ask themselves: *What questions do I need more evidence for?*
- Give students more time to read or annotate, research, and create evidence cards and source cards.

Day 6

- *Mini-lesson:* What is plagiarism and why should we avoid it? (See the TLC "Research Paper Guide" page.) Discuss and explain: *What is the difference between quoting and paraphrasing? Why do I have to cite, no matter which one I do?*
- Model how to paraphrase and quote and cite properly.
- Give students more time to read or annotate, research, and create evidence cards and source cards. *Note:* At this point, no one should be writing *yet*.

Day 7

- *Mini-lesson:* Model developing your thesis argument (see the TLC "Writing 101" page for the Developing Your Thesis Organizer).
- Solicit info from a student to see if anyone is ready to craft a thesis yet: if so, walk the class through another model. If not, identify what they need in order to get to this point.

(*continued*)

(continued)

Days 8 through 20

- Check each student's thesis before he or she begins writing further. Each thesis must be approved.

- Each student should also complete the Unpacking Your Thesis Organizer (see the TLC "Writing 101" page), which is basically a rough outline.

- They may need mini-lessons on how to use evidence cards to organize the paper, how to write from evidence cards, and how to cite sources in the paper (as well as on the Works Cited page).

- Consider allowing time for brief oral presentations of their findings. Audience members can ask questions.

- Here are some helpful Websites:

  This link gives average annual wages of most occupations: http://stats.bls.gov/oes/current/oes_nat.htm

  This is a survey of Sixteen Career Clusters: http://breitlinks.com/careers/career_pdfs/InterestSurvey.pdf

DOGGIE BAG

1. What are the biggest mistakes we typically make when teaching the research paper?

2. What can we do to avoid these mistakes?

3. What do you think your students might struggle with when writing a research paper, and how will you set them up for success?

RESEARCH PAPER TEACHERS' GUIDE

This Research Paper Teachers' Guide (which appears on the TLC "Research Paper Guide" page) explains how to teach the research paper from start to finish and offers additional suggestions about how to help students develop compelling topics within your content area.

Menu

Preliminary Resources for Teachers

Before you launch this paper, check out the following helpful Websites, which will make your life easier.

Academic Integrity at Princeton. This Web-based booklet published by the Office of the Dean of the College at Princeton University, while designed to "[provide] all the information you need about Princeton's academic regulations and how you can safeguard the integrity of your original work," offers an overview of how and why to document sources, along with links to many other writer-friendly Websites.

http://www.princeton.edu/pr/pub/integrity/pages/intro/index.htm

***Research and Documentation Online,* by Diana Hacker and Barbara Fister.** This Web-based book demonstrates how to find and cite sources and provides *sample papers* (available as PDF files) in various disciplines with handy-dandy marginal notes explaining what to do and why.

http://www.dianahacker.com/resdoc

Drudge Report. Though it has a bias in how it features news items, this Website provides valuable links to many major news sources, both national and international.

http://www.drudgereport.com

Introducing the Project

Time frame. How much time you spend on background information depends on the goals of the paper, the goals of the course, and how those goals intersect. Students could spend a month reading a book together or thirty minutes taking notes on a PowerPoint presentation. Establishing the Big Picture might take fifteen to twenty minutes or it might take a whole class period, depending on whether you want students to read and discuss the sample paper(s) you distribute.

Provide *background information* on the topic that everyone in the class analyzes or takes notes on, such as:

- A book
- Historical documents
- A documentary
- A PowerPoint presentation
- Newspaper, magazine, or journal articles
- Several pieces of literary criticism
- An Internet source

Establish *the big picture.* Give students a model of the *end product*—that is, a *sample paper.* While you shouldn't go over every detail of the paper at this stage, you should spend at least a few minutes pointing out some highlights, such as the effective use of topic sentences, parenthetical citations, and the Works Cited list.

Following are two sample papers in MLA format (the Hacker-Fister Website includes other models in other formats at http://www.dianahacker.com/resdoc/) which present opposing arguments on driving and cell phone usage. Marginal notations explain what is done regarding format, content, and organization. *Note:* The first paper (by Levi) also includes a sample outline.

http://dianahacker.com/pdfs/Hacker-Levi-MLA.pdf

http://dianahacker.com/pdfs/Hacker-Daly-MLA.pdf

Be clear with students about where they should store these resources for future reference—either in a section in their notebook or in a special folder for this project.

Developing the Topic and Useful Questions

Students often misconstrue research papers as reports that involve encyclopedias and the dry recitation of facts. They need to understand that research is meant to be not a laundry list, but an investigation, an inquiry-driven process that builds an argument.

Time frame. This question-brainstorming session will probably require an entire class period, and students can type up the questions for homework. Once you've assessed the questions, you might need to intervene with individuals whose questions are ineffective. Showing them the differences between a successful student model (Sample A, which follows) and a weak one (Sample B, which also follows) could help them grasp what they need to do. Alternatively, you could show the whole class both models first, then have them brainstorm on their own.

Explain that this research paper begins with questions *that lead to* arguments *supported by* evidence. Therefore, the best way to start, even if you have given students a broad topic or question to address, is by brainstorming for questions.

Inquiry Phase 1: Develop a Manageable Topic

- If the topic is too broad, this preliminary line of inquiry will help students narrow their focus. *Note:* If students already have a manageable topic, you might want to skip Phase 1 and start with Phase 2.

- **Model the question-brainstorming process.** Using a sample paper as the basis for discussion could enhance students' understanding of how the process looks from start to finish. If you choose this option, start with the broadest topic you can imagine that relates to the final topic and generate questions that become increasingly specific. If the assignment is to write something on safety or technology, you might raise questions such as "What safety- or technology-related issues, concerns, or problems am I most interested in?"

- If you prefer to work from a different topic (one more relevant to your discipline, perhaps), that's fine. The process of using questions to narrow the scope of the topic will be the same.

- **Students should generate ten questions** relating to their broad topic in an effort to narrow the focus. Have them share with a partner, then ask a volunteer to share with the class.

- Once they have arrived at a *manageable topic*, they should be able to *state it in one to two sentences*. Be sure to confirm that they can.

Inquiry Phase 2: Develop Questions Related to the Topic

- Once students have a potentially manageable topic, they should brainstorm on questions relevant to their specific topic, creating twenty questions (but it's early in the process, so they might change their minds about their topic). Explain that this *inquiry-based approach* should drive their research: "You are investigating a topic, looking for evidence with which to build an argument."

- *Note:* If you skipped Phase 1, you should model the question-brainstorming process for Phase 2. You might also want to show them samples of effective and ineffective questions (see Samples A and B, respectively, which follow).

- Have them read these questions to a partner for additional input. While they work on this step, circulate and provide assistance. *Note:* Your discussions with students will serve at least two purposes: (1) to check for understanding and (2) to help students identify where to find answers to some of their questions. Having potential resources in mind will boost their confidence and give them a concrete place to begin their quest.

- Students should type up the questions and turn them in. These questions should guide them in their investigation. Remind students that they should be open to any additional questions that arise.

Sample A Questions

Topic: Consumer Trends in Urban Areas

1. How do urban people spend their money?
2. What are the trends of buying and selling in the urban marketplace?

3. How much of one's salary goes to food and clothing?

4. What are people in urban areas usually able to afford?

5. How well do people in urban areas manage their money?

6. Do they invest any of their money in stocks or other investments?

7. How do the media affect urban consumer trends?

8. How does learning to manage your money help people in urban areas?

9. How much does an average urban person's salary influence spending habits?

10. Are there different spending habits between minority groups?

11. Do people's spending habits cause them to live in urban areas?

12. What can they do differently?

13. How should people from urban areas spend their money wisely?

14. Can people raise themselves from poverty?

15. How do the media influence people's spending habits?

16. How is the economy affected by the spending of poor people who live in cities?

17. Are there trends within certain ethnic groups when spending their money?

18. What would happen to local stores in urban areas if people did not shop there?

19. When gentrification happens, how do people in large cities deal with the higher living costs?

20. Do consumers in the urban marketplace buy more than they sell?

Sample B Questions
(No topic given.)

1. Are they financially stable?

2. Are they materialistic?

3. How do people that come from out of country act?

4. Does the environment affect a child's behavior?

5. How much support do people in poverty have?

6. Are people in this situation satisfied?

7. Why is there a culture of poverty?

8. How many people are employed?

9. What is the employment rate of people over age twenty-one?

10. How many attend college?

11. Is there a culture of poverty?

12. What are some solutions?

13. How does a person's background affect his or her mentality?

14. What percent of people that live in these areas attend school?

15. Are they in gangs or selling drugs?

16. Do they value education?

17. What do those people value?

18. Do they value family?

19. Do some escape this?

20. How long has this gone on for?

Why to Cite

Before teaching students how to find evidence and create evidence and source cards, you should explain *why* citation is necessary. Too often we tell students, "You have to cite, or else it's plagiarism," a sentence that carries no meaning or weight if they don't know what *plagiarism* is. The Academic Integrity at Princeton Website explains why and when to cite and shows several examples of plagiarism (see link given below).

Time frame. The amount of time you spend on this issue will depend on how you want students to process the information (see the sections on Acknowledging Your Sources, *When* to Cite, and How to Avoid Plagiarism, which follow) and how much they already know about it. It might take a whole period to discuss it thoroughly as a class, using the documents that follow. To save class time, you might choose instead to have students read and annotate these documents for homework and the next day give them a quiz and engage in a brief discussion to check for understanding.

Following are helpful excerpts from the Academic Integrity at Princeton Website: http://www.princeton.edu/pr/pub/integrity/pages/intro/index.htm.

Acknowledging Your Sources

There are a variety of reasons for acknowledging the intellectual sources upon which you have built your own work. Below are the key reasons:

- To acknowledge your dependence on another person's ideas or words, and to distinguish clearly your own work from that of your sources.
- To receive credit for the research you have done on a project, whether or not you directly quote or borrow from your sources.
- To establish the credibility and authority of your knowledge and ideas.
- To place your own ideas in context, locating your work in the larger intellectual conversation about your topic.
- To permit your reader to pursue your topic further by reading more about it.
- To permit your reader to check on your use of the source material.

In all of these reasons, the essential element is intellectual honesty. You must provide your reader with an honest representation of your work so that he or she may evaluate its merits fairly. Proper citation demonstrates the depth and breadth of your reading—in effect, documenting the hard work you have put into your research. Proper citation permits a reader to determine the extent of your knowledge of the topic. And, most important, proper citation permits a reader to more readily understand and appreciate your original contribution to the subject. In contrast, a very well-informed, complex, or sophisticated piece of work, without adequate or accurate acknowledgment of sources, will only provoke your reader's concern or suspicion.

Such intellectual honesty is important, not only for your reader, but also for you as the author. For example, you may footnote a paper diligently only to discover that you can hardly find an original idea or sentence of your own. Then you will know you have more work to do in order to develop a substantial original idea or thesis.

Failure to acknowledge the sources—textual, personal, electronic— upon which you have relied is a serious breach of academic integrity. Such

(continued)

(*continued*)

a failure can lead to the accusation of *plagiarism*—defined as the use of any source, published or unpublished, without proper acknowledgment. Plagiarism is a very serious charge, which can result in disciplinary probation, suspension, or expulsion. . . .

The most important thing to know is this: whether you fail to cite your sources deliberately or inadvertently, you will still be found responsible for the act of plagiarism. Ignorance of academic regulations or the excuse of sloppy or rushed work does not constitute an acceptable defense against the charge of plagiarism.

Source: "Academic Integrity at Princeton" (2011), published by the Office of the Dean of the College, Princeton University, is reprinted here with permission. http://www.princeton.edu/pr/pub/integrity /pages/sources

When to Cite

Once students buy into the need to cite, they will have many questions about what exactly should be cited. Again, the Academic Integrity at Princeton Website provides helpful direction about when to cite sources, addressing direct quotations, paraphrasing, summarizing, using facts, information, and data, and supplementary information. (See "When to Cite" at: http://www.princeton.edu/pr/pub /integrity/pages/cite.)

How to Avoid Plagiarism

It will help students to avoid plagiarism if they know what it looks like. See "Examples of Plagiarism" found at: http://www.princeton.edu/pr/pub/integrity /pages/plagiarism.

Time frame. You will save yourself significant aggravation later if you spend time on these examples of plagiarism now.

How to Cite

Even students who see the importance of citing (or at least realize it's required) often fail to see the value of creating note cards for evidence and sources. They view note cards as a waste of time. Your task is to show them how note cards can actually save time, help them stay organized, and help them build a strong argument.

See Evidence Cards versus Source Cards: Models and Rubric in the Appendix of this book and on the TLC "Research Paper Guide" page.

Time frame. The steps for creating evidence and source cards can take more than an hour to cover, depending on how much practice students need. Explaining how to use MLA format for the list of Works Cited (whether you model it with photocopied excerpts from the *MLA Handbook*[1] or by using the super-friendly Website noted later in this section) will probably take at least twenty to thirty minutes. Also, a few days later, after students have found their own sources, you will probably want to give them class time to create evidence and source cards so that you can make sure they're doing things properly.

Give students a sample text (possibly something they've seen before or could use for this paper) and model how to annotate *with questions in mind.* What are the questions they should be asking? Refer back to their brainstormed questions. Remind students, "You are looking for answers to your questions." And again, remind them to be on the lookout for additional questions that occur to them as they read.

Explain how *and* why *to create* evidence cards. Anticipate the problem that some students will want to number their evidence cards sequentially, paying no heed to their source cards. Make sure they see why each evidence card must include its source number. Create a model for students to copy down.

Front of Source Card	Back of Source Card
Argument or Heading Source Number **Either give *opinion*: "The author** **believes …"** **Or give *fact or statistic*: "Four-fifths of** **dentists surveyed …"**	Explain how this evidence supports the argument.

Explain the difference between facts *or* statistics *and* opinions. Both can be evidence, and both need to be cited. Remind them that *common knowledge* does not need to be cited (give examples!), and when in doubt, students should cite.

Explain how *and* why *to create* source cards, *and provide a model.* Students need to know the following:

- The key advantage of using source cards is that students will only have to record the citation information *once*, instead of on every evidence card.

- Creating source cards in MLA format now (note hanging indent on sample below) will save time later.

Front of Source Card	Back of Source Card

Source #
Besthoff, Len. "Cell Phone Use Increases
   Risk of Accidents, but Users Willing to
   Take the Risk." WRAL Online.
   11 Nov. 1999. 12 Jan. 2001
<http://www.wraltv.com/news/wral
   /1999/1110-talking-driving>	

See How and Why to Cite Sources Quiz on the TLC "Research Paper Guide" page.

Parenthetical Citations and Works Cited List

Students often fail to see the logical and logistical connection between parenthetical citations and the Works Cited list. You will have to point this out to them. Be sure to wait for the "Aha!"

See Sample MLA Parenthetical and Works Cited Listings in the Appendix of this book and on the TLC "Research Paper Guide" page.

Time frame. The act of creating a Works Cited list, while seemingly straightforward, has been known to befuddle many students. While the entire class will benefit from an overview of how to use the *MLA Handbook* (and/or a user-friendly Website that serves the same purpose, such as this one, http://www.dianahacker.com/resdoc/p04_c08_s2.html, or the Duke University Libraries Website found at http://library.duke.edu/research/citing) you should probably budget class time—possibly a period—for individual or small-group consultations.

Using a sample paper, explain and demonstrate the relationship between a parenthetical citation and an entry on the Works Cited page. You will literally have to point. Make sure everyone says, "Aha!"

Demonstrate how to use MLA format. Give students a few sample texts to create source cards for. To explain how to cite different kinds of sources, you have at least two options:

Option 1 (print). Use the *MLA Handbook.* Depending on available resources, provide either the whole book or an excerpt with which to practice finding out how to cite various types of sources. It might be useful to photocopy the Electronic Publications section and walk students through how to apply MLA format to a few different kinds of Internet sources.

Option 2 (online). Direct students online to the following Website and walk them through the pull-down menu to learn how to cite different kinds of sources:

> http://www.dianahacker.com/resdoc/p04_c08_s2.html (go to Humanities— Documenting Sources—MLA List of Works Cited)

Finally, check to make sure students understand the different purposes of source cards and evidence cards!

How to *Evaluate* Sources

Although students spend vast amounts of time on the Internet, they are not as savvy as they need to be about evaluating the information they find there.

Time frame. Take a look at the following Web pages and decide how you want students to process them. You could create a whole lesson to check for understanding by providing random printouts of various Internet sources to see how students evaluate them: an opportunity for you to customize this project to suit the needs of your course.

The goal of this lesson is to teach students how to evaluate and cite Internet sources. "How can we tell if a source is valid and reliable? How can we recognize a source's bias, and what should we do about that?" The following Websites address these questions:

Distinguishing Scholarly Journals from Other Periodicals examines four different kinds of periodicals (scholarly, substantive news or general interest, popular, and sensational), explains how to tell them apart, and clarifies which are most useful:

> http://www.library.cornell.edu/olinuris/ref/research/skill20.html

Tips for Evaluating Sources: Evaluating All Sources explains how to evaluate the legitimacy of different Web-based sources—how to check for signs of bias and assess arguments, and what factors to consider when evaluating sources (authorship, sponsorship, purpose, audience, and currency):

http://www.dianahacker.com/resdoc/tips.html

Students should read both of these Websites closely.

How to Find Useful Information

Students will need instruction in how to find useful sources, both online and at the library. Without robust research, their final product will be skimpy at best.

Time frame. This piece requires planning and customized legwork on your part. Reach out to the librarian well in advance, and locate some useful Websites so students will have some leads to follow. Students will probably need at least two hours in the library with your assistance. Giving them Internet search time in class, too, has the added benefit of synergy: when they find helpful Websites, they can share them with the class.

Internet Tips   Anyone can do a Web search for the topic or key words, but students also need to know about relevant Websites. Here is where you should do some customized legwork. The following Websites may help you find links to useful sites:

Drudge Report. Though it has a bias in how it features news items, this Website provides valuable links to many major news sources, both national and international:

http://www.drudgereport.com

Specialized Search Engines and Directories. This Website provides links to sites containing specific information that may not turn up when you do a general search of the Web using Altavista, Yahoo!, and other search engines and directories:

http://webquest.sdsu.edu/searching/specialized.html

Infoplease. This Website provides links to a wide variety of references, such as almanacs, maps, and timelines:

http://www.infoplease.com/index.html

History-Related Resources

American History 102 designed by Professor Stanley K. Schultz of UW-Madison): http://us.history.wisc.edu/hist102/index.html

The Authentic History Center: http://www.authentichistory.com

HarpWeek: Explore History: http://www.harpweek.com[2]

For additional student writing models and guides on how to judge sources, check out Write Source: http://www.thewritesource.com.

Library Tips When using an external library, you should:

- Call the library two weeks in advance to set up a visit.
- Give the librarian a copy of your assignment.

Take students to the library.

- You will probably need at least two hours.
- Make sure students bring library cards.
- Recommend photocopying at the library if necessary (or you can offer to copy things at school if students identify selected passages with sticky notes).

Outlining

Give students a model outline (see http://dianahacker.com/pdfs/Hacker-Levi -MLA.pdf).

- Use the given model or create one based on previously studied material, so they can understand how to do what you're asking without using your ideas directly.
- Outlines should include these elements at a minimum: thesis, topic sentences, and bullet points for evidence.
- Allow some class time and/or office hours for conferring with students on their outlines.

See How to Create an Outline in the Appendix in this book and on the TLC "Research Paper Guide" page.

Final Reminders

Give students a list of clear minimum requirements without which the paper will not be graded.

- Include all steps leading up to the paper's final due date.
- Include the minimum number of pages and sources, and be clear that failure to meet either standard will result in a *zero* (or NGY [No Grade Yet], if you feel generous).

- Allow two weeks between the approved outline deadline and the approved final draft deadline (to ensure that you will have enough time to confer with students).

- Provide additional hints: see How to Avoid Common Research Paper Pitfalls in the Appendix of this book and on the TLC "Research Paper Guide" page.

- *Make each step worth a ridiculously huge grade.* For scoring the paper itself, see Research Paper Rubric in the Appendix of this book and on the TLC "Research Paper Guide" page.

- Remind students to insert page numbers.

- Require students to submit with their final draft all materials they used to write the paper (evidence and source cards, outline, and photocopied sources). Give them manila folders to keep track of everything.

Allow some class time for conferences with students to ensure they are on the right track:

- Meet with individuals or small groups to ensure that they are creating note cards properly.

- Confer with individuals about their proposed theses and topic sentences.

Set up "office hours" so students can see you for extra help.

Note: "Approved" outline doesn't mean "Just turn in any old thing." If the outline is not approved, it is unacceptable and therefore worth *zero*. Remind students not to wait until the last minute to get their outlines approved.

Stick to your deadlines.

DOGGIE BAG

1. Now what do you think your students might struggle with when writing a research paper, and how will you set them up for success? Has your thinking changed?

2. What will *your* research paper assignment look like?

Teaching with Novels

No matter what grade or subject you teach, novels can enrich your students' learning experiences. While novels are traditionally the main dish of the English language arts teacher, other subject areas can also partake of this genre. Students will still learn content, and possibly find it more palatable.

This section looks first at how to teach literary analysis writing and then at how to incorporate novels into history or social studies and science classes.

NOVELS IN ENGLISH LANGUAGE ARTS: LITERARY RESPONSE PAPER WRITING GUIDE

If you're a middle school or high school English teacher, your students probably spend a lot of time reading novels and writing about them. How can you best support your students in this process? The Literary Response Paper Guide (found on the TLC "Literary Response Paper Guide" page) is here to help.

Overview

A literary response paper builds an argument about a text, using evidence to explain how the author uses characters, symbols, or other literary strategies to convey a message.

The typical length is two to three pages (typed, double-spaced, and with a minimum of five paragraphs), but it can be longer. Students should include at least two to three quotes per paragraph, providing context and explanation to illustrate how the evidence supports their arguments.

By the end of their high school careers, students should be able to plan and write a literary response paper on their own, with minimal input from the teacher. Along the way, though, they will need coaching on how to read and write analytically. This guide provides the instructional tools that your students will need to succeed at this task.

Menu

Steps for Success

1. Read *analytically*.
2. Develop a *thesis*.
3. Write the *introduction*.
4. *Unpack* the thesis to create *topic sentences* and an *overall structure*.
5. Find *evidence* to support your topic sentences. Build "*quote sandwiches*," providing *context* and *explanation* for each quote.
6. Write the *conclusion*.

Here are the tools you will need from the TLC "Literary Response Paper Guide" page:

Literary Response Paper Reading Tools
- Generic Annotation Rubrics for Fiction or Narratives and Nonfiction
- Characterization Methods: DDAT
- Character Analysis Organizer
- Character Analysis Organizer Model
- Thinking About Short Stories Questions
- Quotations Chart Sample: *Julius Caesar*
- Symbols Chart Sample: *The Great Gatsby*
- Chapter Notes Organizer
- What's Important Organizer: *Kite Runner* Model
- What's Important Organizer
- Paragraph Responses Sample: *When I Was Puerto Rican*
- Journal Writing Rubric

Literary Response Paper Writing Tools
- Brainstorming for Your Thesis
- Developing Your Thesis Organizer

- Argument versus Evidence: *Catcher in the Rye*
- How to Find the Topic Sentence
- Evaluating Topic Sentences: *I Know Why the Caged Bird Sings*
- Evaluating Topic Sentences: *The Street*
- Paragraph Responses Sample: *When I Was Puerto Rican*
- Unpacking Your Thesis Organizer
- Unpacking Your Thesis Organizer Model
- Essay Outline Organizer
- How and Why to Make a Quote Sandwich
- Give Context and Explanation for Quotes: *Catcher in the Rye*
- Give Context and Explanation for Quotes: *The Bluest Eye*

Steps for Success

1. Read Analytically.

Objectives

- Question the *message, theme, or purpose* of a text.
- Explain the *message, theme, or purpose* of a text.
- Explain how various literary elements fit together to convey this message.

Homework, classwork, and discussion can focus on the following to help students understand that literary elements serve a purpose in the text—to develop and convey the *message or theme.*

Theme

- What topics or issues are addressed in the text, and what argument(s) does the author seem to be making about them?

Characterization or Plots

- What *motives* determine a character's course of action?
- What are the most revealing *aspects* of one of the characters? (Consider his or her thoughts, words, and actions.)

(*continued*)

(*continued*)

- What *external conflicts* affect the main character? (Consider conflicts with other characters, with the setting, and the like.)
- What *internal conflicts* make life difficult for the main character? (Consider the thoughts, beliefs, and ideas that affect the protagonist or one of the other characters.)

Setting
- What *effect* does the setting have on the characters? On the plot? On the theme?

Style
- Are there important *symbols* or *motifs* that add meaning to the novel?
- Does the author employ special techniques (*similes, metaphors,* or *personification*) throughout the work? (What do these elements add to the novel?)
- Is there a specific *mood* or *tone* developed in the novel? How does it add meaning to the novel?
- Are there aspects of the author's *style* or *organization* (such as stream of consciousness, Biblical allusions, multiple points of view, juxtaposition of chapters, narrators, or styles) that enhance the novel's meaning?

Use the following *reading tools* to analyze the text from a variety of angles:

- Generic Annotation Rubrics for Fiction or Narratives and Nonfiction
- Characterization Methods: DDAT
- Character Analysis Organizer
- Character Analysis Organizer Model
- Thinking About Short Stories Questions
- Quotations Chart Sample: *Julius Caesar*
- Symbols Chart Sample: *The Great Gatsby*
- Chapter Notes Organizer
- What's Important Organizer: *Kite Runner* Model

- What's Important Organizer
- Paragraph Responses Sample: *When I Was Puerto Rican*
- Journal Writing Rubric

2. Develop a **Thesis.**   Sometimes a student's understanding of a text will bring a thesis statement immediately to mind, and the student will write it out, then look for quotes or details to prove it. At other times, the exact thesis will not jump out at students, or their first stab at it will be too vague to be effective. In these cases, students might want to look for evidence first, then think about what it will prove.

Objective
- Develop a thesis that is an *argument* (not just a fact from the text, but an opinion that can be supported or refuted through appropriate marshalling of evidence).

Students should be able to construct a fully developed thesis statement. Note that the following samples have at least two parts: *How* an author creates meaning (through character development, conflicts, and symbolism, for example) and *why* (the purpose for doing these things).

Sample Theses

In *The Street*,[1] Ann Petry highlights the conflicts that Lutie has with Boots, Johnson, and Jim to show the difficulty that women, both married and single, have in constructing a life for themselves.

In *The Street*, Ann Petry's characterization of Mr. and Mrs. Chandler underscores the subtle yet pervasive racism that plagues the whole African American community.

One approach to developing a thesis is as follows (see the Developing Your Thesis Organizer on the TLC "Literary Response Paper Guide" page):

- Students *brainstorm* on topics or issues in the text (such as quest for independence; identity; justice; autonomy; challenges of racism, sexism, or classism; learning; risk taking). *Think-pair-share.*

- Students *select* three topics or issues they are most interested in.
- Then ask them to try to *find connections* among these topics and *explain them* in relation to the book (such as "In order to learn and develop our identity, we must take risks; in the process of taking risks, Milkman learns more about who he is").
- *Share to model this thinking process,* which should lead students to draw some conclusions about the *messages* that the author conveys.
- Students identify and share these messages. The "message" is essentially the *conclusion. How* the author achieves or conveys this message is the *thesis.* Students need to consider where they are going with the conclusion as they write the introduction.

Sample Conclusion

Hurston's ultimate message is that while the struggle for equality and independence is arduous, it is a worthwhile and deeply meaningful quest. [*Note:* This is the key element of the conclusion. The rest would be elaboration, such as what follows.] As we confront our own challenges, we can draw hope from Janie's experiences.

Sample Thesis

In *Their Eyes Were Watching God* by Zora Neale Hurston,[2] Janie, the main character, searches for equality and independence, and she learns some important lessons along the way.

Note
- The thesis includes specific details from the book, while the conclusion, which is broader, provides a message *for all of us readers.*
- The thesis should include the author and the title.

Another approach is to use the Brainstorming for Your Thesis handout, as follows:

- *Select a general subject:* the settings of *The Street* (the street itself, Lutie's apartment, Boots's apartment, Junto's bar)

- *Narrow your subject:* use of personification in describing these places
- *Put your thesis in the form of a question:* Why does Petry use so much personification in her description of the various settings of the novel?
- *Compose a final thesis statement:* In *The Street*, Petry's continual use of personification in describing the different places through which Lutie moves indicates both the enormity and the pervasiveness of the social problems ranged against her.

3. Write the Introduction.

Objectives

- Develop an introduction that engages the reader and establishes the argument.
- Provide a compelling, relevant hook; a support statement that connects the hook to the thesis; the thesis; and an additional support statement that extends or elaborates on the thesis.

Once the thesis is written, students will include it in an introduction. The intro should contain a "hook," which pulls the audience into the essay in an interesting way. The hook should creatively introduce some aspect of the thesis, whether it readies the reader to think about the *how*, the literary device or element under consideration, or the *why*, the purpose for the device or the general meaning of the text.

There are several different ways to "hook" a reader into your essay. Try to develop an *image*, find a *quote*, or pose and answer a *question*.

Image

Wiry black hair tops a pair of dull eyes. Stale breath mingles with the rasping sounds emanating from a thin-lipped mouth. Sturdy feet clomp along the side of a road. This may sound more like a creature from the latest science fiction movie than a woman who invites sonnets to be written about her beauty. However, in William Shakespeare's Sonnet 130, "My Mistress' Eyes Are Nothing Like the Sun,"[3] several surprises are in store for the reader. Shakespeare uses the traditional sonnet form and references to conventional Elizabethan beauty to create a nontraditional celebration of love.

(continued)

(*continued*)

Quote

"It is not beauty that endears, it's love that makes us see beauty," notes Leo Tolstoy. Though writing more than two hundred years before Tolstoy, William Shakespeare captures this same sentiment in Sonnet 130, "My Mistress' Eyes Are Nothing Like the Sun."[4] Through the use of the traditional sonnet form and references to conventional Elizabethan beauty, Shakespeare celebrates his love for his mistress. His lines convince the reader to see love despite the lack of the usual signs of beauty.

Question

Who can define beauty? It is an elusive quality, but a question that has been posed throughout the ages and across a variety of cultures. Consequently, the concept changes with each attempt at definition, but remains a desirable subject for contemplation within many works of literature. William Shakespeare, in his Sonnet 130, "My Mistress' Eyes Are Nothing Like the Sun,"[5] struggles to define the attractiveness of the woman he loves. His use of the traditional sonnet form and references to conventional Elizabethan beauty ultimately give way to an understanding of beauty that rests on his love for his mistress instead of her physical appearance.

The hook should be followed by one or more sentences in which the connection between the hook and the thesis is explained.

4. Unpack *the Thesis to Create* Topic Sentences *and an* Overall Structure.

Objectives

- Identify key provable points in the thesis.

- Create argument-based topic sentences derived from these provable points, typically answering the questions *How?* and *Why?*

Complete the Unpacking Your Thesis Organizer (see the Unpacking Your Thesis Organizer Model). The first box asks for your thesis or argument statement. Think of your thesis as the A in your journey from A to Z. In the case of a literary response paper, you want to combine your message with the author, the title, and the strategies or names of characters being used to convey the message.

To develop topic sentences, *you need to ask* How? *(in other words, "What does it look like?") and* Why? *(that is, "What causes this situation?") for each part (in the most logical order)*. When writing about characters, it can also be helpful to ask, "What does the character learn?" The responses to these questions will become your topic sentences. Here are some examples of questions that could lead to topic sentences:

- Why does Janie have to search for equality?
- How does Janie search for equality?
- How successful is she, and why? What does she learn?
- Why does Janie have to search for independence?
- How does Janie search for independence?
- How successful is she, and why? What does she learn?

The body paragraphs should begin with a topic sentence to prove the thesis (or some aspect of a multi-dimensional thesis) and to preview the content of the paragraph.

Like the thesis statement, topic sentences in a response paper should be arguments, not facts or overly broad statements:

Inappropriate (fact): Old Tom Joad is the head of the family, and is called on to make decisions for the members when necessary. (This is obvious; it simply restates factual events from the plot.)

Inappropriate (too broad): Men think they are smarter than women.

Appropriate (argument): Old Tom Joad is the head of the family, but the decisions he makes indicate that he is no longer fit for that role. (This is an argument; someone could argue against it and prove the opposite—that he *is* the best person for that role.)

Note: Because understanding the functionality of topic sentences is so important, teachers may want to review and utilize the following materials:

- Argument versus Evidence: *Catcher in the Rye*
- How to Find the Topic Sentence

- Evaluating Topic Sentences: *I Know Why the Caged Bird Sings*
- Evaluating Topic Sentences: *The Street*
- Paragraph Responses Sample: *When I Was Puerto Rican*

See the following additional *writing tools*:

- Unpacking Your Thesis Organizer
- Unpacking Your Thesis Organizer Model
- Essay Outline Organizer

5. Find Evidence to Support Your Topic Sentences; Build "Quote Sandwiches," Providing Context and Explanation for Each Quote.

Objectives
- Select relevant evidence to support each topic sentence.
- Build "quote sandwiches": provide effective context for quotes, including setup and explanation.

Students who have read analytically and annotated well should possess enough familiarity with details of the text to be able to locate and select suitable quotations to support their arguments. They may need to be reminded to look back at all of the reading tools they used, as well, to find appropriate evidence.

It is a good idea to review once again the difference between *argument* and *evidence* (see Argument versus Evidence: Catcher in the Rye).

Use How and Why to Make a Quote Sandwich and Give Context and Explanation for Quotes: *Catcher in the Rye* or Give Context and Explanation for Quotes: *The Bluest Eye* to explain how to provide effective context and explanation for quotes.

Body paragraphs should include "quote sandwiches," which include the quote and the necessary accompanying sentences:

Point. Give the argument being addressed.

Quote and context. The quote needs to be set up with context (who is speaking or being addressed, why, when, where, and so forth). The quote should fit seamlessly into a sentence. Teach students how to employ the ellipsis or bracketed clarification to make the quote and sentence flow. *Example:* "'One way,' [Lutie] echoed. Yes, a one-way ticket, she thought. I've had one since the day I was born" (434).[6]

Comment or analysis. Explain how this specific quote proves the point. Focus on the entire quote selected and the exact diction used in the quote to explicate it fully.

There should be transitions between the different quotation sandwiches and between paragraphs. Transitions can be words (such as *similarly* or *in addition*) or ideas ("Steinbeck continues to highlight the migrants' struggle by . . .")

See the following additional *writing tools*:

- Argument versus Evidence: *Catcher in the Rye*
- How and Why to Make a Quote Sandwich
- Give Context and Explanation for Quotes: *Catcher in the Rye*
- Give Context and Explanation for Quotes: *The Bluest Eye*

6. Write the Conclusion.
Objective

- Create a conclusion that conveys the author's ultimate message and how it relates to readers.

The conclusion should bring the ideas of the text "out into the world." It should show readers why they should care about the message, and/or bring the essay "full circle" back to its hook or starting point. *Note:* Though it is based on the thesis, it does not merely restate the thesis. It should address the *implications* of the thesis.

Sample Conclusion

Hurston's ultimate message is that while the struggle for equality and independence is arduous, it is a worthwhile and deeply meaningful quest. As we confront our own challenges, we can draw hope from Janie's experiences.

How should you grade this essay? See the "Essay Writing Rubric" and other resources on the TLC "Writing Rubrics" page for more insights about grading papers.

DOGGIE BAG

1. What is the purpose of a literary response paper, and what skills does it require?

2. Which aspects of writing a literary response paper do you think your students might struggle with, and how will you set them up for success?

USING NOVELS IN HISTORY, SOCIAL STUDIES, AND SCIENCE

While it's fairly obvious to English teachers how students should write about novels, it's less clear to history, social studies, and science teachers how their students should use them. This isn't to say that it shouldn't be done.

The hardest part of using novels in content areas other than English is selecting appropriate books. The second-hardest part is figuring out what students should do in response to their reading. Let's look at each issue more closely.

Phase 1: How to Select Novels

Here are some vital questions to address when selecting novels for your content-area students:

- **Do you know what level(s) your students are reading on?** If you already possess reading-level data on your students, great. If not, one option is to employ the McLeod Assessment of Reading Comprehension (available on the TLC "Guided Reading" page and also at http://www.newtunings.com/57 /data/Grade.Level.Tools/HS.English/McLeod.Read.Comp.pdf), which assesses reading comprehension with the "cloze" (fill-in-the-blank) technique and only takes fifteen minutes to administer to an entire class. The results will give you a rough idea of where each student is and help identify appropriate levels to target. Depending on your school's access to resources, you might purchase several sets of titles for students who fit into leveled reading groups. *Hint:* Use www.lexile.com to find titles on students' levels.

- **What do you want students to learn about the topic from reading the book?** If you want to use the novel as a way to introduce historical or scientific content, identify your specific objectives. This list will help you narrow the choices. Again, the "search" function on www.lexile.com can help you find books on particular subjects.

- **Do you want everyone in the class to read the same book, or do you want students to have options?** It might make sense to do a classwide novel first, so that you can teach key content and reading strategies to all of your students simultaneously. But then you should really consider giving students a choice about what to read next. When they are allowed to choose, they tend to be more invested in the decision. Choice enables you to provide more differentiated instruction, as well. So consider reading groups.

Phase 2: How Should Students Respond to the Novel?

In content areas other than English, your curriculum probably does not require you to teach students how to write literary response papers, so you have more flexibility in how they respond to novels in your class. Make sure you review the sections in Chapter Two on before-, during-, and after-reading strategies (especially the description of RAFT). Also, check out the TLC "Analyzing Literature" page for a variety of ways to unpack novels, including the Character Analysis Organizer and What's Important Organizer. Here are some additional options:

- **Journal responses.** Design open-ended or inference questions for students to respond to. Check out the Journal Writing Rubric on the TLC "Writing Rubrics" page.

- **Paragraph responses.** Create topic sentences for which students write the rest of the paragraph, providing evidence from the text. See Paragraph Responses Sample: *When I Was Puerto Rican* on the TLC "Analyzing Literature" page.

- **Socratic Seminars.** See the Socratic Seminars Made Easy section in Chapter Four. If students are all reading the same book, this method can be especially effective; you can run seminars after they have read each chapter, major chunks, or the whole book.

- **Book Talk Projects.** See the section on Book Talk Projects in Chapter Four. This approach works best if students are all reading different books (to avoid repetition). Students deliver a brief description about the book, then respond to questions from the audience. *Note:* For a novel, you can use the Book Talk Project for Class Novel.

- **Last but not least, *be creative.*** Students can write letters from historical figures to the characters in their books. Or they can write letters of recommendation for entrance into some particular Hall of Fame for one of their characters. Or you can create a way for students to report out on key historical or scientific insights or information that they have drawn from the book. Consider the RAFT (Role, Audience, Format, Topic) approach described in Chapter Four. Don't be afraid to use your imagination! Your students will appreciate the challenge.

DOGGIE BAG

1. What should you consider when planning to use novels in history, social studies, or science classes?

2. How might you use novels in your class?

Desserts

This section includes, naturally, a scrumptious recommended reading list and the Appendix, where you'll find a handful of extra-sweet resources.

Recommended Reading

I present this recommended reading list in honor of my dear late friend David Mallery, a great mentor throughout my teaching career, who said that life was too short "so we should always order two desserts." A mutual friend once described David as being "determined to inspire every teacher within the sound of his voice," and I have no doubt that he had that impact on me. I first met David a few months into my rookie year. He could see that I was barely treading water, and with great compassion, he helped me to reflect on what had brought me into the pool—my admiration for some amazing teachers I'd been lucky to have and my determination to do something meaningful with the excellent education I'd received—and then he kept encouraging me, through countless letters and phone calls (and, on several delightful occasions, dinners with multiple desserts) to "keep at it."

I think David would love being referenced in this chapter not only because of his passion for cakes and pies and root beer floats, but also because of his deep respect for educators and his abiding appreciation for people who create inspirational works: plays, movies, songs, books . . . I know he would love this collection of resources that have inspired and helped me. I hope you will, too.

ON READING AND VOCABULARY

Beck, Isabel L., Margaret G. McKeown, and Linda Kucan. *Bringing Words to Life: Robust Vocabulary Instruction.* New York: Guilford Press, 2002.

Beers, Kylene. *When Kids Can't Read: What Teachers Can Do.* Portsmouth, NH: Heinemann, 2003.

Calkins, Lucy, and Kathleen Tolan. *A Guide to the Reading Workshop: Grades 3–5.* Portsmouth, NH: Heinemann, 2010.

Daniels, Harvey, and Steven Zemelman. *Subjects Matter: Every Teacher's Guide to Content-Area Reading.* Portsmouth, NH: Heinemann, 2004.

Gallagher, Kelly. *Deeper Reading: Comprehending Challenging Texts, 4–12.* Portland, ME: Stenhouse, 2004.

Hart, Betty, and Todd R. Risley. *Meaningful Differences in the Everyday Experiences of Young American Children.* Baltimore: Paul H. Brookes, 2002 (3rd printing of original 1995 book).

Harvey, Stephanie, and Anne Goudvis. *Strategies That Work: Teaching Comprehension for Understanding and Engagement* (2nd ed.). Portland, ME: Stenhouse, 2007.

Keene, Ellen O., and Susan Zimmerman. *Mosaic of Thought: The Power of Comprehension Strategy Instruction* (2nd ed.). Portsmouth, NH: Heinemann, 2007.

Lattimer, Heather. *Thinking Through Genre: Units of Study in Reading and Writing Workshops 4–12.* Portland, ME: Stenhouse, 2003.

Miller, Donalyn. *The Book Whisperer: Awakening the Inner Reader in Every Child.* San Francisco: Jossey-Bass, 2009.

Robb, Laura. *Teaching Reading in Social Studies, Science, and Math: Practical Ways to Weave Comprehension Strategies into Your Content Area Teaching.* New York: Scholastic, 2003.

Tovani, Cris. *I Read It, but I Don't Get It: Comprehension Strategies for Adolescent Readers.* Portland, ME: Stenhouse, 2000.

Trelease, Jim. *The Read-Aloud Handbook* (6th ed.). New York: Penguin, 2006.

Zwiers, Jeff. *Building Academic Language: Essential Practices for Content Classrooms, Grades 5–12.* San Francisco: Jossey-Bass, 2008.

ON WRITING

Anderson, Carl. *How's It Going? A Practical Guide to Conferring with Student Writers.* Portsmouth, NH: Heinemann, 2000.

Anderson, Jeff. *Mechanically Inclined: Building Grammar, Usage, and Style into Writer's Workshop.* Portland, ME: Stenhouse, 2005.

Atwell, Nancie. *In the Middle: New Understandings about Writing, Reading, and Learning* (2nd ed.). Portsmouth, NH: Heinemann, 1998.

Caine, Karen. *Writing to Persuade: Minilessons to Help Students Plan, Draft, Revise, Grades 3–8.* Portsmouth, NH: Heinemann, 2008.

Calkins, Lucy. *The Art of Teaching Writing.* Portsmouth, NH: Heinemann, 1986.

Calkins, Lucy, and Marjorie Martinelli. *Launching the Writing Workshop.* Portsmouth, NH: Heinemann, 2006.

Dorfman, Lynne R., and Rose Cappelli. *Mentor Texts: Teaching Writing Through Children's Literature, K–6.* Portland, ME: Stenhouse, 2007.

Fletcher, Ralph. *What a Writer Needs.* Portsmouth, NH: Heinemann, 1993.

Graff, Gerald, and Cathy Birkenstein. *They Say/I Say: The Moves that Matter in Academic Writing* (2nd ed.). New York: Norton, 2010.

Lattimer, Heather. *Thinking Through Genre: Units of Study in Reading and Writing Workshops 4–12.* Portland, ME: Stenhouse, 2003.

Noden, Harry R. *Image Grammar: Using Grammatical Structures to Teach Writing.* Portsmouth, NH: Heinemann, 1999.

ON CURRICULUM AND INSTRUCTION

Bambrick-Santoyo, Paul. *Driven by Data: A Practical Guide to Improve Instruction.* San Francisco: Jossey-Bass, 2010.

Lemov, Doug. *Teach Like a Champion: 49 Techniques That Put Students on the Path to College.* San Francisco: Jossey-Bass, 2010.

Wiggins, Grant, and Jay McTighe. *Understanding by Design* (2nd ed.). Alexandria, VA: ASCD, 2005.

ON HOW WE THINK ABOUT TEACHING, LEARNING, AND CHANGE

Coyle, Daniel. *The Talent Code: Greatness Isn't Born. It's Grown. Here's How.* New York: Random House, 2009.

Dweck, Carol. *Mindset: The New Psychology of Success.* New York: Random House, 2006.

Heath, Chip, and Dan Heath. *Switch: How to Change Things When Change Is Hard.* New York: Broadway Books, 2010.

Appendix

See the following items:

11–12 ELA Common Core Standards Tracking Spreadsheet Excerpt

Evidence Cards versus Source Cards: Models and Rubric

Sample MLA Parenthetical and Works Cited Listings

How to Create an Outline

How to Avoid Common Research Paper Pitfalls

Research Paper Rubric

11–12 ELA Common Core State Standards Tracking Spreadsheet Excerpt[1]

		CPI code	Unit 1	Unit 2	Unit 3	Unit 4	Unit 5	Unit 6
Reading Standards for Literature								
Key Ideas and Details								
1	Cite strong and thorough textual evidence to support analysis of what the text says explicitly as well as inferences drawn from the text, including determining where the text leaves matters uncertain.	RL.11–12.1						
2	Determine two or more themes or central ideas of a text and analyze their development over the course of the text, including how they interact and build on one another to produce a complex account; provide an objective summary of the text.	RL.11–12.2						
3	Analyze the impact of the author's choices regarding how to develop and relate elements of a story or drama (e.g., where a story is set, how the action is ordered, how the characters are introduced and developed).	RL.11–12.3						

Name _____ Date _____

Evidence Cards versus Source Cards: Models and Rubric

Front of Evidence Card	Back of Evidence Card
Argument or Heading Source Number **Either give *opinion*: "The author believes … "** **Or give *fact/statistic*: "Four-fifths of dentists surveyed … "**	Explain how this evidence supports the argument.

Your cards received: _____ /10

Comments:

_____

_____

_____

Front of Source Card	Back of Source Card
Source # Besthoff, Len. "Cell Phone Use Increases Risk of Accidents, but Users Willing to Take the Risk." WRAL Online. 11 Nov. 1999. 12 Jan. 2001 <http://www.wraltv.com/news/wral /1999/1110-talking-driving>	

Your cards received: _____ /10

Comments:

_____

_____

_____

Source: From Evidence Cards versus Source Cards: Models and Rubric on the TLC "Research Paper Guide" page.

Sample MLA Parenthetical and Works Cited Listings[2]

Type of Source	Parenthetical Citation	Works Cited Listing
Book	Fleming addresses the causes of the American Revolution (23).	Fleming, Thomas. *Liberty! The American Revolution.* New York: Viking, 1997.
Newspaper article (in print)	Under Maryland law, he could only find the defendant guilty of negligent driving and impose a $500 fine (Layton C1).	Layton, Lyndsey. "Legislators Aiming to Disconnect Motorists." *Washington Post* 10 Dec. 2000: C1+.
Online journal article	The California Highway Patrol opposes restricting cell phone use while driving, claiming that distracted drivers can already be prosecuted (Jacobs).	Jacobs, Annette. "Guest Opinion: No New Laws Needed for Driver Distractions." *Wireless Week* 24 May 1999. 12 Mar. 2001 <http://www.wirelessweek.com/News/May99/gopn524.htm>.
Online research report (without individual author)	In 2000, researchers at the Harvard Center for Risk Analysis found that the risks of driving while phoning were small compared with other driving risks. Whereas the cell phone user's chances of dying are about 6 in a million per year, someone not wearing a seatbelt has a risk of 49.3 per million, and someone driving a small car has a risk of 14.5 per million (3).	Harvard Center for Risk Analysis. "Cellular Phones and Driving: Weighing the Risks and Benefits." Risk in Perspective July 2000. 15 Mar. 2001 <http://www.hcra.harvard.edu/pdf/July2000.pdf>.

Name _____ Date _____ Team _____

How to Create an Outline[3]

Complete the following steps to create a working outline for your research paper. Remember: while completing this task, you may realize that you have more research to do concerning your argument.

Steps

1. Sort your *evidence cards* into rough topics or categories. If you were writing about the American Revolution, for example, "Colonists Who Revolted against the British" might be a category.

2. Create an argument or heading for each of your topics or categories. Taking the example of the paper about the American Revolution, you would transform the category "Colonists Who Revolted against the British" into "John Adams was a key leader in the American Revolution" as an *argument* you could prove.

3. Category analysis:

   What do we know?

   Why is this important?

   What does this have to do with _____?

4. If you have any empty categories, it means that you need to continue to find sources.

5. Put your categories in a logical order—the order that you will be addressing them in your paper.

How to Avoid Common Research Paper Pitfalls[4]

1. Provide Sufficient Context for Quotes or Paraphrase Evidence

Problem: As many may not be aware, there is pollution inside buildings and homes. There are several agents that are responsible for this indoor pollution. "Tobacco, smoke, cooking and heating appliances, and vapors from building materials, paints, furniture, etc. cause pollution inside buildings" (source 11).

Solution:

_____

_____

_____

_____

_____

2. Avoid Using "I" and "You" or "Your" Statements

Problem: Some cars are better on gas mileage, others are made safer, while others are just equipped with more gadgets for entertainment. These upgrades may make the car more efficient for your pocket and make your ride more enjoyable, but what they are not upgraded for is the environment.

Solution:

_____

_____

_____

_____

_____

(continued)

How to Avoid Common Research Paper Pitfalls (*continued*)

Problem: Cell phones help you keep in contact with your friends and also come equipped with tons of games that can be played when you are not talking on the phone. In my opinion, a cell phone is a substitute for a house phone for when you want to be away from your house talking with someone.

Solution:

_____

_____

_____

_____

_____

3. Cite the Source Appropriately

Problem: "MySpace going mainstream also attracts unwanted attention"(source 1).

Problem: "Tobacco, smoke, cooking and heating appliances, and vapors from building materials, paints, furniture, etc. cause pollution inside buildings" (source 11).

Solution:

_____

_____

_____

_____

_____

Research Paper Rubric[5]

Name:	/100	Assignment: Research Paper
Writing Standards	**Points**	**Comments**
Introduction Hook One to two supporting statements Thesis argument Thesis support statement	/20	
Topic Sentences Transition from previous paragraph Argument for the paragraph that answers *how* and *why* in response to the thesis	/10	
Evidence Use accurate factual information to provide detailed support to prove thesis and topic sentences, including: Context surrounding quote (who, what, where, when, and why) Quote or paraphrase (at least two per body paragraph) Explanation of quote and how it illustrates or proves the point Sources (at least five different sources)	/40	
Conclusion Draw logical, thoughtful conclusions and/or make reasonable predictions Summarize the argument and reveal an insight		
Proper MLA Citation Format Parenthetical citations in proper format Works Cited page in proper format		
Length requirement of _____ pages.	/10	
Overall Persuasion, Coherence, and Depth of Analysis Build convincing paragraphs and an overall argument that flows clearly Make thoughtful, logical, and substantial inferences throughout the paper Anticipate potential counterarguments to the thesis Find meaningful connections	/30	
Grammar and Word Choice Use language well (sophisticated vocabulary, subject-verb agreement, and present tense) Punctuate properly Structure sentences effectively	/10	
Total		**Total points** $\times$ 2 =

N O T E S

CHAPTER ONE

1. Beers, K. (2003). *When kids can't read: What teachers can do*. Portsmouth, NH: Heinemann, p. 45.

2. Lemov, D. (2010). *Teach like a champion: 49 techniques that put students on the path to college*. San Francisco: Jossey-Bass, pp. 35–41.

3. Fitzgerald, F. S. (2003). *The great Gatsby*. New York: Scribner. (Originally published 1925)

4. Gallagher, K. (2004). *Deeper reading: Comprehending challenging texts, 4–12*. Portland, ME: Stenhouse, pp. 2–3.

5. Sedaris, D. (2000). *Me talk pretty one day*. New York: Little, Brown.

6. Dostoyevsky, F. (2004). *The idiot*. (C. Garnett, trans.) New York: Barnes & Noble.

7. Hart, B., & Risley, T. R. (2002, 3rd printing of original 1995 book). *Meaningful differences in the everyday experiences of young American children*. Baltimore: Paul H. Brookes.

8. Hart & Risley, pp. 197–198. *Note:* Children from professional families would hear 45 million words; from working-class families, 26 million; and from welfare families, 13 million.

9. Hart & Risley, p. 176. *Note:* Specific data: 86 to 98 percent.

10. Walker, D., Greenwood, C., Hart, B., & Carta, J. (1994). Prediction of school outcomes based on early language production and socioeconomic factors. *Child Development, 65*, 606–621.

11. Hart & Risley, pp. 58–59.

12. Beers, pp. 15–16.

13. Miller, D. (2009). *The book whisperer: Awakening the inner reader in every child*. San Francisco: Jossey-Bass, pp. 24–25.

14. Davis, R. Personal communication via e-mail, Sept. 11, 2011.

15. Handout developed by Jessica Majerus and Katy Wischow.

16. Truss, L. (2003). *Eats, shoots, and leaves*. New York: Gotham Books, pp. 9–10.

17. Anderson, J. (2005). *Mechanically inclined: Building grammar, usage, and style into writer's workshop*. Portland, ME: Stenhouse.

18. Noden, H. R. (1999). *Image grammar: Using grammatical structures to teach writing*. Portsmouth, NH: Heinemann.

19. Harris, G. (2011, January 22). Federal research center will help develop medicines. *New York Times*. Retrieved from http://www.nytimes.com/2011/01/23/health/policy/23drug.html?emc=eta1

20. Erlanger, S. (2011, January 22). Talks on Iran's nuclear program close with no progress. *New York Times*. Retrieved from http://www.nytimes.com/2011/01/23/world/middleeast/23nuke.html?emc=eta1

21. Lemov, p. 47.

22. Hosseini, K. (2003). *The kite runner*. New York: Riverhead Books.

23. See the TLC "Comprehension 101" page for the complete document.

24. Available on the TLC "Writing Rubrics" page.

25. Lemov, pp. 158–159.

26. Available on the TLC "Comprehension 101" page.

27. Available on the TLC "Comprehension 101" page.

28. Gardiner, J. R. *Stone Fox*. New York: Scholastic, 1980, p. 53.

29. Available on the TLC "Analyzing Literature" page.

30. Retrieved from http://deoxy.org/emperors.htm

31. Hart & Risley.

32. Beck, I. L., McKeown, M. G., & Kucan, L. (2002). *Bringing words to life: Robust vocabulary instruction*. New York: Guilford Press, p. 3.

33. Beck, McKeown, & Kucan, p. 4.

34. Beck, McKeown, & Kucan, p. 5.

35. Beck, McKeown, & Kucan.

36. Beck, McKeown, & Kucan, p. 37.

37. Beck, McKeown, & Kucan, pp. 15–16.

38. Wischow, K. Personal communication via e-mail, Jan. 24, 2012.

39. Beck, McKeown, & Kucan.

40. Available on the TLC "Building Robust Vocabulary" page.

41. Available on the TLC "Building Robust Vocabulary" page.

42. Wiesel, E. (2006). *Night*. (M. Wiesel, trans.) New York: Hill and Wang. (Originally published 1958)

43. See the TLC "Connecting Reading, Writing, and Test Prep" page.

44. Salinger, J. D. (1991). *The catcher in the rye*. Boston: Little, Brown. (Originally published 1945)

45. Wischow, K. Personal communication via e-mail, Jan. 24, 2012.

46. Homer. (2007). *The Iliad*. (W.H.D. Rouse, trans.). New York: Penguin Group.

47. "Self-Reliance," Emerson's Texts, assessed August 28, 2012, http://www.emersoncentral.com/selfreliance.htm

CHAPTER TWO

1. Trelease, J. (2006). *The read-aloud handbook* (6th ed.). New York: Penguin, p. 4.

2. Trelease, pp. 8–9.

3. Beers, K. (2003). *When kids can't read: What teachers can do*. Portsmouth, NH: Heinemann, pp. 220 ff.

4. Lemov, D. (2010). *Teach like a champion: 49 techniques that put students on the path to college*. San Francisco: Jossey-Bass, p. 276.

5. Lemov, p. 280.

6. Available on the TLC "Analyzing Literature" page.

7. Miller, D. (2009). *The book whisperer: Awakening the inner reader in every child*. San Francisco: Jossey-Bass, pp. 24–25.

8. Beers, pp. 15–16.

9. Miller, pp. 27–29.

10. Miller, p. 30.

11. Davis, R. Personal communication via e-mail, Sept. 11, 2011.

12. Shakespeare, W. (2004). *Romeo and Juliet*. New York: Simon & Schuster.

13. See http://www.fountasandpinnellleveledbooks.com for more information.

14. Miller, p. 46.

15. Miller, p. 50.

16. Beers, p. 16.

17. Beers, p. 122.

18. Daniels, H., & Zemelman, S. (2004). *Subjects matter: Every teacher's guide to content-area reading*. Portsmouth, NH: Heinemann, p. 100.

19. Keene, E. O., & Zimmerman, S. (2007). *Mosaic of thought: The power of comprehension strategy instruction* (2nd ed.). Portsmouth, NH: Heinemann, pp. 72 ff.

20. Beers, p. 101.

21. Tovani, C. (2000). *I read it, but I don't get it: Comprehension strategies for adolescent readers*. Portland, ME: Stenhouse, p. 65.

22. Lemov, pp. 287–288.

23. Shakespeare, W. (2003). *Macbeth*. New York: Simon & Schuster.

24. Chiger, S. Personal communication via e-mail, July 13, 2011.

25. Discussed in the following sources: (1) Daniels & Zemelman, pp. 104–105. (2) Robb, L. (2003). *Teaching reading in social studies, science, and math: Practical ways to weave comprehension strategies into your content area teaching*. New York: Scholastic, pp. 101–105.

26. Robb, pp. 110–112.

27. Lemov, pp. 137–141.

28. Lemov, p. 140.

29. Lemov, p. 285.

30. Discussed in the following sources: (1) Beers, pp. 74–80; (2) Robb, pp. 114–116; (3) Daniels & Zemelman, pp. 108–109.

31. Beers, pp. 77–78.

32. Travers, P. L. (2006). *Mary Poppins*. New York: Houghton Mifflin Harcourt. (Originally published 1934)

33. Robb, pp. 105–107.

34. Lemov, pp. 111–125.

35. Tovani, pp. 36–37.

36. Tovani, pp. 35–36.

37. Tovani, p. 51.

38. Trelease, J. (2006). *The read-aloud handbook* (6th ed.). New York: Penguin, p. 23.

39. Trelease, p. 9.

40. Trelease, pp. 75–80.

41. Harvey, S., & Goudvis, A. (2007). *Strategies that work: Teaching comprehension for understanding and engagement* (2nd ed.). Portland, ME: Stenhouse, pp. 48–49.

42. Harvey & Goudvis, p. 48.

43. Beers, p. 123.

44. Daniels & Zemelman, p. 102.

45. Beers, p. 124.

46. Beers, p. 124.

47. Gallagher, K. (2004). *Deeper reading: Comprehending challenging texts, 4–12.* Portland, ME: Stenhouse, pp. 59–60.

48. Gallagher, pp. 58–59.

49. Keene & Zimmerman, pp. 100–101.

50. Harvey & Goudvis, pp. 102–104.

51. Dweck, C. (2006). *Mindset: The new psychology of success.* New York: Random House.

52. Available on the TLC "Nonfiction Reading Strategies" page.

53. Available on the TLC "Nonfiction Reading Strategies" page.

54. Available on the TLC "Nonfiction Reading Strategies" page.

55. Harvey & Goudvis (p. 56; see also pp. 55–59), citing Harvard College Library. (2007). "Interrogating Texts: 6 Reading Habits to Develop in Your First Year at Harvard." Harvard University. http://hcl.harvard.edu/research/guides/lamont_handouts/interrogatingtexts.html

56. Robb, p. 185. See also pp. 186–187.

57. Harvey & Goudvis, p. 135.

58. Daniels & Zemelman, p. 106.

59. Dweck.

60. Beck, I. L., McKeown, M. G., & Kucan, L. (2002). *Bringing words to life: Robust vocabulary instruction*. New York: Guilford Press, pp. 16–20.

61. Daniels & Zemelman, pp. 134–135.

62. Gallagher, p. 118.

63. Hurston, Z. N. (1998). *Their eyes were watching God*. New York: Perennial Classics. (Originally published 1937)

64. Gallagher, pp. 118–119.

65. Atwell, N. (1998). *In the middle: New understandings about writing, reading, and learning* (2nd ed.). Portsmouth, NH: Heinemann, p. 90.

66. Lattimer, H. (2003). *Thinking through genre: Units of study in reading and writing workshops 4–12*. Portland, ME: Stenhouse.

CHAPTER THREE

1. Shakespeare, W. (2003). *Hamlet*. New York: Simon & Schuster.

2. Retrieved from http://deoxy.org/emperors.htm

3. Available on the TLC "Writing 101" page.

4. Seuss, Dr. (1957). *How the Grinch stole Christmas!* New York: Random House.

5. Fletcher, R. (1993). *What a writer needs*. Portsmouth, NH: Heinemann, p. 4.

6. Lemov, D. (2010). *Teach like a champion: 49 techniques that put students on the path to college*. San Francisco: Jossey-Bass, pp. 71–74.

7. Cofer, J. O. (1995). *An island like you: Stories of the barrio*. New York: Penguin Books.

8. Santiago, E. (1993). *When I was Puerto Rican*. New York: Random House.

9. Available on the TLC "Writing 101" page.

10. Seuss.

11. Hurston, Z. N. (1998). *Their eyes were watching God*. New York: Perennial Classics. (Originally published 1937)

12. Petry, A. (1991). *The street*. New York: Houghton Mifflin. (Originally published 1946)

13. Available on the TLC "Writing 101" page.

14. Dorfman, L. R., & Cappelli, R. (2007). *Mentor texts: Teaching writing through children's literature, K–6*. Portland, ME: Stenhouse, p. 12.

15. Coyle, D. (2009). *The talent code: Greatness isn't born. It's grown. Here's how.* New York: Random House, p. 2. *Note:* Coyle is referring to a study conducted by Australian music psychologists Gary McPherson and James Renwick, who tracked Clarissa's progress for several years.

16. Coyle, p. 4.

17. Coyle, p. 105.

18. Coyle, p. 16.

19. Lemov, pp. 71–74.

20. Dorfman & Cappelli, pp. 12–13.

21. Anderson, C. (2000). *How's it going? A practical guide to conferring with student writers*. Portsmouth, NH: Heinemann, p. 130.

22. Anderson, pp. 130–132.

23. Dorfman & Cappelli, p. 15.

24. Calkins, L. (1986). *The art of teaching writing*. Portsmouth, NH: Heinemann, pp. 170–171.

25. Lattimer, H. (2003). *Thinking through genre: Units of study in reading and writing workshops 4–12*. Portland, ME: Stenhouse, pp. 12–13.

26. Calkins, L., & Martinelli, M. (2006). *Launching the writing workshop*. Portsmouth, NH: Heinemann, pp. 2–8. *Note:* Others, such as Kristen Painter and Carl Anderson, use slightly different terminology for the same structures.

27. Calkins & Martinelli, p. 19.

28. Fletcher, R. (1993). *What a writer needs*. Portsmouth, NH: Heinemann, pp. 13–19.

29. Anderson, p. 17.

30. Anderson, p. 20.

31. Calkins, p. 149.

32. Anderson, p. 27.

33. Anderson.

34. Calkins & Martinelli, p. 99.

35. Lemov, pp. 210–213.

36. Daily Writing Tips found at http://www.dailywritingtips.com/punctuation-saves-lives

37. Truss, L. (2003). *Eats, shoots, and leaves.* New York: Gotham Books, pp. 9–10.

38. Anderson.

39. Anderson, p. 23.

40. Retrieved from http://www.goodeatsfanpage.com/humor/otherhumor/dog_cat_diary.htm

41. Available on the TLC "Writing Rubrics" page.

42. Available on the TLC "Writing Rubrics" page.

43. Chiger, S. Personal communication via e-mail, Jan. 24, 2012.

44. Wiggins, G., & McTighe, J. (2005). *Understanding by design* (2nd ed.). Alexandria, VA: ASCD.

CHAPTER FOUR

1. Lemov, D. (2010). *Teach like a champion: 49 techniques that put students on the path to college.* San Francisco: Jossey-Bass, pp. 111–125.

2. Dweck, C. (2006). *Mindset: The new psychology of success.* New York: Random House.

3. Lemov, p. 47.

4. Heath, C. & Heath, D. (2010). *Switch: How to change things when change is hard.* New York: Broadway Books, p. 183.

5. Heath & Heath, p. 228.

6. Lemov, p. 204.

7. Lemov, pp. 163–165.

8. Lemov, pp. 111–125.

9. Lattimer, H. (2003). *Thinking through genre: Units of study in reading and writing workshops 4–12.* Portland, ME: Stenhouse, pp. 36–39.

10. Lemov, p. 92.

11. Lemov, pp. 92–97.

12. Lattimer, p. 12.

13. Zwiers, J. (2008). *Building academic language: Essential practices for content classrooms, grades 5–12.* San Francisco: Jossey-Bass, p. 198.

14. Zwiers, p. 117.

15. Check out http://www.jeffzwiers.com/resources.html for Academic Language Posters.

16. Zwiers, p. 145.

17. Zwiers, p. xiii.

18. Morrison, T. (1987). *Song of Solomon*. New York: Penguin Group. (Originally published 1977)

19. Zwiers, p. 143.

20. Zwiers, p. 144.

21. Wiesel, E. (2006). *Night*. (M. Wiesel, trans.) New York: Hill and Wang. (Originally published 1958)

22. Available on the TLC "Socratic Seminars" page.

23. Available on the TLC "Socratic Seminars" page.

24. Available on the TLC "Socratic Seminars" page.

25. Available on the TLC "Socratic Seminars" page.

26. Available on the TLC "Socratic Seminars" page.

27. Available on the TLC "Book Talk Project" page.

28. Available on the TLC "Book Talk Project" page.

29. Available on the TLC "Book Talk Project" page.

CHAPTER FIVE

1. Graff, G., & Birkenstein, C. (2010). *They say/I say: The moves that matter in academic writing* (2nd ed.). New York: Norton, p. xix.

2. Graff & Birkenstein, pp. 24–25, among many others.

3. Caine, K. (2008). *Writing to persuade: Minilessons to help students plan, draft, revise, grades 3–8*. Portsmouth, NH: Heinemann, p. 202.

4. See variations on the TLC "NJ ASK Prep" and "NJ HSPA Prep" page.

CHAPTER SIX

1. Beck, I. L., McKeown, M. G., & Kucan, L. (2002). *Bringing words to life: Robust vocabulary instruction*. New York: Guilford Press, p. 8.

2. Bambrick-Santoyo, P. (2010). *Driven by data: A practical guide to improve instruction*. San Francisco: Jossey-Bass, pp. 251–255.

3. Lattimer, H. (2003). *Thinking through genre: Units of study in reading and writing workshops 4–12*. Portland, ME: Stenhouse.

4. Lattimer, p. 4.

5. Lattimer, p. 13.

6. Available on the TLC "Writing Rubrics" page.

CHAPTER SEVEN

1. Retrieved from http://www.literacycookbook.com/page.php?id=122

2. Wiggins, G., & McTighe, J. (2005). *Understanding by design* (2nd ed.). Alexandria, VA: ASCD, p. 106.

CHAPTER EIGHT

1. Gibaldi, J., & Achtert, W.S. (Eds.). (1984). *MLA handbook for writers of research papers* (2nd ed.) New York: Modern Language Association of America.

2. Many thanks to Mitch Brenner at KIPP-Infinity Charter School for these leads!

CHAPTER NINE

1. Petry, A. (1991). *The street*. New York: Houghton Mifflin. (Originally published 1946)

2. Hurston, Z. N. (1998). *Their eyes were watching God*. New York: Perennial Classics. (Originally published 1937)

3. Shakespeare, W. (1998). *Shakespeare's sonnets* (K. Duncan-Jones, Ed.). London: Arden Shakespeare, p. 375.

4. Shakespeare, p. 375.

5. Shakespeare, p. 375.

6. Hurston, p. 434.

7. Hurston.

APPENDIX

1. Excerpted from K–12 ELA Common Core Tracking Spreadsheet on The Literacy Cookbook Website (URL: http://www.literacycookbook.com /page.php?id=138), which was adapted from the Common Core Standards (URL: http://www.corestandards.org/the-standards/english-language-arts -standards).

2. Citations from the sample MLA document on Diana Hacker's Website (http://dianahacker.com/pdfs/hacker-daly-mla.pdf). Available on the TLC "Research Paper Guide" page.

3. Available on the TLC "Research Paper Guide" page.

4. Available on the TLC "Research Paper Guide" page.

5. Available on the TLC "Research Paper Guide" page.

INDEX

Brown, E., 100

Building Academic Language: Essential Practices for Content Classrooms (Zwiers), 17, 121–122

Bulleted details, 39

C

Calkins, L., 79, 99, 101

Calling on students, 115

Cappelli, R., 95, 97

Carta, J., 12

Categorizing information, 56

Celebrations, 117

Character traits, 27–28

Characterization, 193–194

Charisma, of teachers, 6

Checking for understanding, 73

Chiger, S., 56, 111

Choice, of text, 52–53, 203

Choral pronunciation, 120–121

Citing sources: online resources for, 178; process of, 184–186; purpose of, 182–184; works cited list for, 186–187

Class discussions: in academic language, 122; logistics of, 123–124; paraphrasing of, 21; reading assessments and, 74; Socratic Seminars for, 125–135; in Think-Pair-Share activity, 59

Classroom management: discussions and, 123; making inferences and, 23; workshop approach and, 78

Clauses, 17

Climbing the Comprehension Process Stairs theory, 7–11

Cloze reading, 157

Clustering information, 56

Cofer, J. O., 90

Cold-calling strategy, 118

Collaboration, culture of, 101–102, 117

Collective identity, 117

Common Core Standards: curriculum revision of, 160; emphasis on nonfiction in, 48; evidence and argument in, 38; tracking sheet for, 2, 38, 212; Website for, 2

Common knowledge, 185

Common language, 121

Compelling writing, 96

Complete sentences: for effective speaking and listening, 119; expressing main arguments as, 38; lack of, in student responses, 116

Compositional risks, 146

Comprehension: background knowledge and, 11–13; definition of, 7; importance of, 2–3, 7, 45; inferencing skills and, 22–28, 37–42; key reading skills critical to, 13–42, 75; literacy's link to, 7; paraphrasing and, 13–21; for test preparation, 150; theories about, 7–11; vocabulary skills and, 28–36. *See also specific comprehension strategies*

Concentration, lack of, 60

Conclusion, 196, 201

Conferences, writing: to provide feedback, 88; for research papers, 190; in writing workshop, 100–101

Confused readers, 60

Connections, making: background knowledge and, 64; as during-reading strategy, 64; graphic organizers for, 64

Constructive feedback, 126

Content areas: making inferences in, 22; visualizing strategy in, 69

Context: misleading, 30; in quote sandwiches, 200–201; test-taking tips and, 157–158; for vocabulary assessment, 36; for vocabulary instruction, 28–36, 122

Copying sentences, 103

Coyle, D., 96

Creativity, 204

Curriculum: design considerations of, 74–75; overwhelming nature of, 1–2; recommended reading for, 208; textbook as, 71

D

Daniels, H., 62, 69, 76

Davis, R., 15, 29, 51

DBQ. *See* Document-Based Questions approach

DEAR. *See* Drop Everything and Read

Decoding. *See* Phonics

Deep practice, 96

Deeper Reading (Gallagher), 11

Developing/dependent readers: definition of, 50; paraphrasing and, 13; support for, 51

Dictionaries, 31

Differentiated instruction: for different types of readers, 50–51; in K–8 instruction versus secondary instruction, 53

Direct context, 30

Direct instruction, 122

Discussion leaders, 123

Discussions. *See* Class discussions

M

Macbeth (Shakespeare), 56

Main argument, 38

Main idea: in comprehension process theory, 10; definition of, 38; in fiction versus nonfiction, 48; instruction in, 37–42; test-taking tips for, 156–157; versus topics, 37–38

Main idea questions, 150, 154

Majerus, J., 33, 34

Martinelli, M., 99

McKeown, M. G., 30, 31, 33

McLeod Assessment of Reading Comprehension, 203

McPherson, G., 96

McTighe, J., 111, 166

Me Talk Pretty One Day (Sedaris), 11

Mechanically Inclined: Building Grammar, Usage, and Style into Writer's Workshop (Anderson), 17, 103

MeeGenius, 46

Mentor texts: description of, 95–96; effective use of, 96–97; mini-lessons and, 99; in writing conferences, 100

Mentor Texts (Dorfman & Cappelli), 95

Metaphors, 83–84

Middle school students, 14

Miller, D., 50, 51, 53, 79

Mini-lessons: description of, 99; in genre study approach, 99; for research papers, 174–176; versus Your Turn lessons, 97

Misdirective context, 30

MLA Handbook, 178–179, 185–187

Modeling: of academic language, 122; to brainstorm research questions, 179–180; to build fluency, 46; of dramatic reading, 46; as during-reading strategy, 61–62; of group work reports, 124; mentor texts for, 95–97; writing, 87

Monitoring comprehension: modeling of, 62; process of, 60–61; students' inability to, 59–60

Monty Python and the Holy Grail (film), 21

Morrison, T., 123

Motivation, of students: mentor texts and, 96; reasons for lack of, 1

Motivational grammar, 102–104

Myers, W. D., 118

Mystery Envelope strategy, 76–77

N

New Jersey Assessment of Skills and Knowledge, 161

Night (Wiesel), 126

No Child Left Behind, 149–150

Noden, H., 17

Nonfiction: annotation rubric for, 66; Book Talk Projects in, 136–138; genres of, 47–48; idioms in, 18; importance of, 48; inferring main idea of, 48, 156; locating main idea in, 37–38

Note cards, 184–186

Note taking: during Book Talk Projects, 139; as during-reading strategy, 62; for effective speaking and listening, 120; in Socratic Seminars, 125, 126, 131

Novel selection, 202–204

Novels. *See* Fiction; Literary response writing

O

Open-ended responses, 161–163

Opinions, 185

Oral fluency, 115–117

Outlines, 189

Ownership, of learning, 52–53

P

Page numbers, 190

Paragraph responses, 204

Paraphrasing: automatic use of, 13; in class discussions, 21; in comprehension process theory, 8–9; description of, 13; for effective listening and speaking, 118; instructional strategies for, 19–21; lack of background knowledge and, 11–12; versus making inferences, 23–24; needed vocabulary for, 12; required skills for, 14; steps for teaching, 14–21; versus summarizing, 41; test question design and, 151–152

Parenthetical citations, 186–187

Parents: explanations of, 12–13; logical thinking and, 13; role of, in reading instruction, 45; vocabulary of, 12; workshops for, 45, 61

Partner reading, 46

Periodicals, 187–188

Persistence, in reading, 63–64

Personal narratives, 48, 156

Persuasive writing: description of, 145; organization of, 147–148; preparing students for, 146–148; purpose of, 82–83; Socratic Seminars on, 128; traits of effective, 145–146

Petry, A., 90, 93, 195

Phonics: goal of, 46; online resources for, 46; teacher's role in, 45–46

Phrases, instruction in, 17

Physical education, 166